Just Don't Call Me MA'AM

HOW I DITCHED THE SOUTH,
FORGOT MY MANNERS,
AND MANAGED TO SURVIVE MY TWENTIES
WITH (MOST OF) MY DIGNITY STILL INTACT

Anna Mitchael

SEAL

Just Don't Call Me Ma'am
How I Ditched the South, Forgot My Manners, and Managed to Survive My
Twenties with (Most of) My Dignity Still Intact

Copyright © 2010 by Anna Mitchael

Published by
Seal Press
A Member of the Perseus Books Group
1700 Fourth Street
Berkeley, California

Library of Congress Cataloging-in-Publication Data

Mitchael, Anna.
 Just don't call me ma'am : how I ditched the south, discovered the
wide world of bikini waxes, and managed to survive my twenties with
(most of) my dignity still intact / by Anna Mitchael.
    p. cm.
  ISBN-13: 978-1-58005-316-7
  ISBN-10: 1-58005-316-5
  1. Women--United States--Social conditions. 2. Feminism--United
States. I. Title.
  HQ1421.M58 2010
  305.242'2092--dc22
  [B]
                                          2009034642

9 8 7 6 5 4 3 2 1

Cover and interior design by Kate Basart/Union Pageworks
Printed in the United States of America by Edwards Brothers
Distributed by Publishers Group West

Contents

For my mother, who let me leave without letting me go.

Introduction

I've been called a lot of names in my twenty-nine years of living. Daughter, friend, enemy, brat, girlfriend, partner, confidante, compadre, liar, genius, cynic, liberal, goddess, and, of course, the oldie but goodie (and still quite effective): boy, you're a stubborn pain-in-the-ass.

And that list is just the tip of the Popsicle stick.

Of all the names I've been called, however, none bothered me quite as much as the one that escaped the lips of the cutest, sweetest, most all-American-looking teenage grocery checker when he focused his innocent eyes on me and asked, "Would you like paper or plastic, *ma'am*?"

Immediately, the color drained out of my rosy, red—previously thought to be youngish—cheeks. I looked left and saw no one. To the right—nobody there either. Behind me . . . nope, no ma'am in sight. I looked back at the young clerk, who was very obviously waiting for an answer: I was the ma'am in question.

I wanted to head for the exit—with or without my soy milk and sushi. Once I cleared the doors, I reasoned, I could simply run back to the days when I was young enough to shotgun beers with seventeen-year-old guys, when I knew more about the politics of a sorority house than a corporate office, when I was more worried about making curfew than getting crow's feet.

But there is no turning back time. And perhaps more important, one should never underestimate the potential a spicy sushi roll has to totally turn your day around.

So I did what any self-respecting ma'am would do. I held my head high and told the young gentleman that I preferred paper. Then I slid my sunglasses on to shield my aging eyes from the sun and walked very gingerly to my car, protecting my fragile joints at every step.

When I got home, I crumpled into a tiny ball on my living room floor and waited for night to come and steal another sliver of my youth.

And then my cell phone rang.

Because it was close enough that I didn't have to uncurl from the fetal position to pick it up, I answered the call. On the other end of the line my grandmother's voice rang through loud and clear.

"Anna," she said, in the authoritative way that she speaks when she is about to tell me she's shipping me a pecan pie and I am to eat every slice as soon as it arrives, or that she believes it's time for me to visit Texas for a couple days so we can sit on her front porch swing.

"Yes ma'am?" I answered on autopilot.

And then my grandmother snapped at me. "Don't call me ma'am," she said. "I had enough trouble getting used to being a grown-up—and ma'am just makes me feel like an old lady."

"You're right Grandma, I'm sorry," I said. Here I was, defeated by the words of the grocery-store clerk, yet I was willing to throw that same stone at my dear grandmother. *Perhaps I deserve the wrinkles,* I thought. Maybe the crow's feet would be karmic retribution for all those years I spent innocently saying ma'am, not knowing the damage it was doing to another.

"I've got news," she said.

"Okay," I answered.

"It took me seventy years, but for the first time in my life I have finally figured out how to get the same dimensions as Dolly Parton."

This was not the news I was expecting.

"How, Grandma?" I asked.

I heard her take a sip of her iced tea before answering. I could imagine her on her swing, enjoying a lazy, summer day.

"It was easy, really," she said. "I learned how to do a handstand."

There will be time for being a ma'am. Yes, there will be time. Just like there will be time for sleep. And a time to give up the fight against gravity and slide on that one ugly but oh-so-comfortable pair of cotton underwear that stretches all the way up to your belly button, sucking in your stomach while simultaneously repelling any possibility for a sexual encounter. That time will be when I'm six feet underground.

Grocery-store baggers of The United States of America, consider yourselves warned. You can call me a bitch, a diva, a hussy, or a ho.

Just don't call me ma'am.

Chapter 1

Call Me a Grown-Up

You wake up and assume it will be a Saturday like any other Saturday. You will lie in bed and pretend to be asleep while he starts his day. You will keep your eyes closed and imagine his thoughts. Most likely a debate on what he wants for breakfast. What's he considering? It's Saturday, so he's in the mood for pancakes. To cook them here, at the apartment, or to go to a restaurant? It might cross his mind that he should skip pancakes and only drink coffee. After all, that paunch has started to take on the more permanent look that transforms tummies to bellies.

Yes, he would think about that, but then he would resist letting that concern throw his plans for breakfast off course.

You wonder if he is considering waking you for Saturday morning sex, but you realize you no longer know his thoughts well enough on that subject. You hear him hurl his foot off the bed to hit the wood floor—those hardwoods you so loved when the two of you first found the apartment.

A brownstone in Brooklyn.

A yuppie paradise.

Paradise lost, you think. Then you laugh, quietly, but audibly, at your own joke. This laughter exposes your charade of sleep.

"You awake?" he asks. You keep your eyes closed.

"Yes," you answer.

When you open your eyes you expect to see him stepping into the bathroom, but instead he is in front of the closet that you share. He has his red duffel bag, the one he packs for weekend trips to Vermont and work trips (more frequently lately, it seems). The sight of the bag surprises you because there is no trip planned.

No, no trip, not that you can recall.

You wonder if you've forgotten something. If another piece of information has joined that group that so frequently slips through the cracks these days. No longer limited to birthdays of your college friends and the zip code of your last apartment. Now spontaneous weekend trips that might return the two of you to Paradise are shadowing the dust bunnies in your brain.

"What's up with the bag?" you ask. While you've been contemplating the declining state of your memory, he's stepped into jeans and dropped a sweatshirt over his head. There were socks on his feet already and now he's stepping into his favorite sneakers, the ones you always vaguely thought were trying a little too hard to be cool.

Instead of answering your question about the bag he asks if you will get out of bed so that the two of you can talk.

You have an inkling of a much larger thought: This Saturday will not be like other Saturdays. That knowledge arrives slowly, like the reveal of a crime scene in a movie. First you see the empty room, then the foot over the bathtub. You are at the mercy of others, though—the camera guy, the director, the screenwriter. You have no choice but to be as patient as you can be (nothing says out-of-control bitch like a woman your age throwing a tantrum) and wait for the story to be revealed at the pace that the human being delivering it sees fit.

You answer him by getting up. Your jeans are on the floor at the foot of the bed but you don't feel like formalizing this talk by dressing up, so you find sweatpants and slide them on. You may not be in the driver's seat, don't have a say about this talk, but you will keep one piece of control: the clothes that touch your skin.

He picks up the duffel bag, which is packed. From where you laid in bed, you hadn't noticed it was already full. You follow him through the short hallway to the living room. You pass pictures on the wall of times when you appeared to be happy, very happy. Paradise.

Your living room looks as it did when you left it the night before. On the coffee table is a book with spine spread open, pages down, and an inch of wine sitting in a green goblet—where did you get that goblet? Was it a leftover from an apartment one of you lived in before? The product of a shopping spree after you moved in together?

You wonder whether he would notice if you drank the wine now.

How long has it been since you talked to him? Scratch that. How long has it been since you had a conversation with him? Something other than an interesting (enough) article in *The New York Times* or what his mother would like the two of you to do for Thanksgiving. (See her, of course.)

You imagine he will begin this talk in about twenty seconds, as soon as both of you have chosen a position in the room. Before those twenty seconds pass, you are going to have to acquire some

CALL ME A GROWN-UP

nerves of serious steel. The wine would help with that. You stare at it. But instead of taking the last sip, you sit on your overpriced and understyled Pottery Barn sofa. The two of you had agreed it was the least-Pottery-Barn-looking sofa offered at Pottery Barn. You wonder why that had ever seemed important, not being the type of couple who shopped there. Both of you were willing to ignore so many other things that actually mattered.

He opens his mouth and the talk begins.

He's leaving, he says. Going to his sister's on the Upper West Side. Your first thought is that you never liked his sister. Next you process his words and realize this talk is most likely going to end with termination of the relationship. As you are trying to under-stand what this means for life as you know it, you return to your first thought and realize, *Well, maybe I'll never have to see his sister again.* Your nerves of not-anywhere-near-steel-at-this-moment are thank-ful for the distraction of that silver lining.

You ask some questions.

How long has he been planning this departure?

How sure is he?

He has been sure for a while, he says.

A while.

You think about the vagaries of this term. There was the sushi dinner last Sunday night. He was bored with his beer, bored with you. More tangible than the taste of raw tuna was the feeling of rejection. It lingered for days.

A while.

A year ago there was the ten-day trip to Rio de Janeiro when the two of you did not have sex. Not once. His sister was living in Rio then. You remember how small you felt every time her eyes jumped over you in her fancy living room. That was a while ago.

A while.

He has nothing left to say and you have no more questions to ask so he picks up his duffle bag and stands in the middle of

JUST DON'T CALL ME MA'AM

the room. You have an inkling of the pain to come, like when you realize the killer is still in the room. He has not left, and the camera guy, the director, the screenwriter are in danger for having moved closer to the dead leg. The whole story is revealed: Everyone will hurt.

At that moment you hate him for leaving, but you hate yourself more for not having left first. You contemplate whether you could beat him to the door. Your duffle bag is not packed, though, and you don't have a sister with a place on the Upper West Side where you can stay. For a second you find yourself disappointed that you don't have a sister at all, though this seems a strange thought to have now, when you've never felt that longing before. You remain seated. He keeps standing in the center of the room.

"I'll call you?" he says and asks at the same time.

You realize that sentence is as confused as this situation has become. He will have to call. The belongings will have to be split. The rent will have to be paid.

You think about your grandmother's warning when the two of you moved in together, that people don't buy cows when they get milk for free. At the time you resented being compared to a cow, and why couldn't she understand that both of you had made the decision together.

But both of you had not made *this* decision together. You would be the one left, he the leaver. Even if your grandma had given the advice for all the wrong reasons, you still wish you had listened.

You know that the right thing to do is to stand up and hug him, because even though this is the man breaking your heart, he's also the man who's spent every day for the last eighteen months in a bathroom with Anthropologie prints hanging on the wall, simply because you liked them there. He's the man who once took a road trip with you across Montana, a state so wide and free it was impossible not to feel as though anything was possible.

He's the man you once imagined getting old with, in a pair of rocking chairs on a Southern porch. Even though dragging him to the South just for a visit was always more trouble than it was worth.

You sigh. You stand. You hug. He awkwardly releases you as though you are a body he does not know. You have hugged twice-removed step cousins that way, and coworkers after an especially excessive happy hour—hugs that are given because initially it feels like the right thing to do but once you are halfway into the embrace, everybody involved knows they've stepped too far over the line of intimacy.

You sigh again. And you feel the tears coming.

You don't want him to see you cry.

You don't yet know that at the end of the week you will call him in tears. And again the week after that.

You will cry when he brings you back your lamp.

And when he passes the restaurant you are sitting in with friends, even though he doesn't see you inside.

Oh you will cry. You will sob. The rage of rejection will burn more strongly than the rational realization that him leaving might be the best thing that could happen to you.

And he does leave. He backs out the door. Backs out on the idea that Paradise might still be here. He backs out on the IKEA furniture you lugged from New Jersey together. On the piece of art you bought him when you were visiting your parents in Malaysia. On the goblet of unknown origin. You, the cow who foolishly gave the milk for free, have been left, holding back tears.

When you hear him close the door that leads from the brownstone to the street you know you are truly alone. This Saturday will be different than any other Saturday because you will be on your own in the world. Worse than that, on your own in this massive city. But that isn't what starts the tears. You begin to cry when you realize you've already been alone for more days than you had been willing to admit. Even to yourself.

People walk down your street talking loudly, dogs bark, the weather takes another tiny tiptoe to winter but your world, for hours, does not move. You surprise yourself with the duration of this stillness. You remain seated on the couch until you realize you're sitting there because you are waiting to see if he will come back. But he is not going to do that.

He has been sure.

For a while.

You aren't ready for the outside world. You do not call your mother or your best friend. You do not throw rocks at the window of the guy who lives in the apartment that backs up to yours, so that he will walk to his window, notice you sitting alone, and bear witness to your personal tragedy.

No, you do what any person searching for warm comfort in the face of personal tragedy would do. You order Chinese food. You order two of everything—you don't even want the neighborhood Chinese restaurant to know your change in relationship status. When the deliveryman arrives at your door you thank him by name. Jose has been delivering Chinese food to you for the last six months.

You consider that you and Jose have things in common, things you never contemplated before this day. He probably left where he grew up to seek out another part of the world for a better existence. What would "better" mean to Jose? More pay? What did "better" mean to you when you left the South? Independence? Freedom from the idea that you had to marry young, have children quickly, develop an interest in Bunko?

Standing at your doorway in dirty sweatpants, no makeup and red eyes, paying for double on the dumplings and kung pao shrimp even though you will be dining alone, it occurs to you that this might be the time to get flexible with your definition of "better."

Your phone is ringing, so you say goodbye to Jose, close the door, lock it, and hook the chain. By the time you reach the phone it has stopped ringing, but when you look at the missed call, you see it wasn't your ex. (Oh God, did you just think that, has your mind already found the truth in what you haven't even said out loud?)

The caller was your best friend, but you can't tell her, not yet, not while the dumplings are still hot in the white Styrofoam container that kills the earth but gives the doughy outer shell so much warm love. These dumplings might hold the only happiness of your whole day. You return to the couch. You eat. You leave the empty containers next to the wine glass. You think it's probably not a good idea to take that last sip of wine.

But then you do it anyway.

After all, you are heartbroken. Wine in the middle of the day is an inalienable right for the heartbroken everywhere. This thinking could get you in trouble down the road. But now you can't even see where down the road might be. The road you thought you were on has just dead-ended in an apartment in Brooklyn, many states away from the solace of the South. You miss your friends and family, and smart desserts like bourbon balls, where the alcohol is already added inside, so that the heartbroken can numb their pain at any time of day in a more clandestine fashion.

You finally reach for the phone, but not to tell anyone the news. Instead you call your grandmother and ask her to recite her recipe for Texas chili. It's a cold day, you say, even though you don't know that for sure. You can see the wind bending the trees but you haven't felt the air. You remind her that you love to make chili for dinner when it's cold. The tacit understanding is that you're cooking for two, but you never actually say that. So you're not lying, not exactly. She delivers the recipe and then she reminds you to be wary of canned jalapeños, it's better to find them fresh. Then she backs up, because she remembers your (ex-) boyfriend doesn't like spicy food. She says that she guesses you can skip the jalapeños altogether, if you must.

You have a piece of paper and a pen but you haven't written down a word. You listen as she details numbers of tomatoes and dashes of cumin, but all you can think about is being alone for the rest of this Saturday.

Probably for Sunday.

Possibly forever.

You don't want to be alone on a Saturday, not like this, not as someone who was left.

And so you cry. Hard. And harder. You know this probably isn't easy on your grandmother, but you can't stop, not even long enough to explain to her why you are crying.

She asks what is wrong, over and over again, in a way that breaks your heart to hear, because her voice gets smaller and less sure every time she asks and you feel as though this is a direct result of the miles between you somehow stretching and expanding, and being farther away is the last thing you need.

I'm not hanging up the phone, she finally says, until you tell me what's going on.

Not Hanging Up The Phone is a big damn deal in your grandmother's world. She does not have call-waiting and so Not Hanging Up The Phone could easily translate to Missing The Call She's Been Waiting For All Her Life. You have seen the worry in her eyes when she stays on the phone too long. Who might be calling right now? Could Publishers Clearing House be lost and in need of directions to my front door?

You say something along the lines of, "I think he left me."

"You think," she asks, "or you know?"

"I know," you answer. "He is sure."

She sits on this announcement for a second. You take this opportunity to draw a few sharp breaths and let oxygen reenter the equation of your body chemistry.

CALL ME A GROWN-UP

"I am sorry you are hurting, but I never much liked that man," she says rather calmly. "I always hoped there would be another love for you."

You think about this while your tears wind down. About all your friends who have rings and strollers, a set of tiered items they acquire that represent the forward-momentum of their lives. You wonder how you will look at starting over as a step forward, how you will ever find a way to prove to the world that really, you will be better off with another love, or maybe even alone.

It occurs to you that the world may not care. Maybe all you need to do is find a way to believe it yourself.

And your grandma knows much more of moving on than you do.

She knows more about living than you do.

Even though you do not know for sure, you imagine that at some point in her life she has felt the hand that reaches up into a heart, breaks it open, and then continues northbound where it will wrap the brain in a fist of fear.

You have no choice but to believe what she says.

"Yes ma'am," you say in a show of deference to her wisdom. Out of respect. But you have said the wrong thing, you know this immediately.

"I understand that you're having an extraordinarily bad day," she answers. "But I've told you before, when you call me ma'am it makes me feel like an old lady. And I didn't even like being a grown-up, much less an old lady."

For a moment you feel guilty because she has told you that before. You think you understand. "I feel tired, too, Grandma, and old," you say.

She starts to laugh, "Oh no, no you don't. You don't know the first thing about feeling like an old lady. In fact, the way I see it, today might be the first day you are finally in reach of being a grown-up."

You speak for a few more minutes, you assure her you will be fine and that you will call friends to come over and be with you. Then the two of you hang up. You are still alone.

Your state of being alone will not change until two days later when you finally call your mother, who is not at her home in Malaysia, but vacationing in Amsterdam. When you tell her the news, she leaves the Van Gogh Museum in a cab for the airport and buys a ticket to JFK. She only has three days of clothes packed, but of course, she does not mention that inconvenience. Finally, you call your best friend, who comes over and sits with you until your mother arrives.

It is not an easy time. But you do not forget what your grandmother said. She wants you to love again. You are not old, you have no right to be tired, you are just beginning. And under no circumstances—not even near-mental breakdown due to relationship meltdown—will "ma'am" ever be considered a term of endearment when there are still years of (possibly irreverent) living to come.

The road had not dead-ended. It had just taken an unexpected curve. If only I could have seen then that it was taking a much-needed turn in the right direction.

CALL ME A GROWN-UP

Chapter 2

Call Me
an Adventurer

I f you live in Texas and you are sane, you loathe the approach
of summer. Like the drive to the gynecologist's office, when
the only things standing between you and the silver stirrups are a
couple miles of road and a parking lot, a Southern summer leaves
you with no choice but to keep your foot on the gas, grin, and
bear it.

Hundred-degree temperatures.

Zero wind.

Roadkill baking on the side of the highway until it's so over-
done that even the crows speed up when they pass by.

However, junior high girls are not sane. They are petite creatures with hormones that start off steady and slow—*pop . . . pop . . . pop*—and then, for reasons imperceptible to the outside eye, speed into a *popopopopop* that can't be controlled.

I know all about the volatility of being a junior high girl. Before my discoveries of makeup and mischief (which happened at separate times, much to the chagrin of Bible-study leaders who warned that eye shadow was the gateway habit to larger, more problematic habits like oral sex), I was a junior high girl. I waded deep in swampy trenches of adolescence with the hormones cookin', the moods swingin', the whole kit and (all of my mom's old makeup I could fit in the) caboodle.

And back in those days—when I was a junior high girl living in Texas—I welcomed summer like it was the second coming of Santa Claus.

The pleasures of the season were more plentiful than the New Kids on the Block posters hanging above my bed. Summer art programs, where I would transform piles of used Popsicle sticks into sticky wood cabins with severe architectural flaws. Trips to the mall, where the arctic air conditioning lulled me into thinking, *Why yes, the smartest purchase I could make with my allowance is a pair of fall boots!,* even though the only shoes I would wear for the next two months were a pair of flip-flops.

There were swim teams and slumber parties and—because we did not yet know that the moles on our bodies could turn on us—weeks of laying on bright beach towels in the Bermuda grass of our backyards.

As if those pleasures did not make for a perfect picture of ecstasy, around the middle of summer, for one week that usually fell at the end of July or the beginning of August, my parents would drive me out of the Houston suburb where we lived and drop me in East Texas for a week of Camp Grandma.

For the first twelve years of my life, Camp Grandma was the most important week of my year. I got to sleep as late as I wanted in the double bed that had my great-grandmother's bedspread laid across it. Then I would wake up and get to drive my grandma down to the country mart in the golf cart that she and my grandpa used to get around their small retirement community. When I was really young, I sat in her lap and steered; later she would sit in the passenger seat and keep one hand on the wheel. Eventually, full command of the cart was mine.

At the country mart she would buy things that Texans need to replenish on a daily basis, like Crisco, and I would start my day with a blue Slushee drink so that on the way back to her house I could wave at the other retired folks who passed us by and flash my big, blue smile—a kind reminder to those aging souls that while dentures were not always a walk in the park, the grass wasn't always greener on the other side.

Our afternoons were spent playing games and watching TV, and when my grandfather got home from the golf course, he would teach me to play pool.

Other people had the kinds of grandmas who baked cookies with you, and grandpas who sat you in their laps and told inspirational stories about the Great Depression. My grandpa encouraged my success with a plastic Minnie Mouse poolstick, and I don't remember a time when anyone could touch a thing in my grandma's kitchen without her looking as though she'd like to take a billiard stick to the back of their heads—and not of the plastic Minnie Mouse variety.

Of course, in the current age of family collapse and tumultuous upbringings, to complain about your grandparents pimping you into a young beer-maiden or insisting that you sit to the side and eat the fruits of their labors instead of burning your hands on hot coals while you knead bread is like saying that having sex with Brad Pitt would be, like, okay, *I guess.*

I missed out on the sleep-away camps other girls went to, but I don't regret one day I spent at Camp Grandma. I didn't learn any songs or sit around any fires or make best friends forever with a cabinmate who would become a pen pal, then float away into the oblivion, only to mysteriously resurface as a friend on Facebook two decades down the road. There were none of the "typical" camp experiences. But for that one week of the year, whatever room I was in, whatever I was doing, whatever I was eating, someone was making sure that I was happy and content and taken care of. I was the star of the show. I was the apple of the (and I say this with more love than eight hundred Hallmark cards smooshed into one sentiment could express) cataracts in my grandparents' eyes.

I loved every spoiled second.

It was a different kind of love that ended up bringing my excitement for Camp Grandma to a close. This love arrived in the summer of my twelfth year. It was intense, it was soulful, and every time I thought about the love my heart would *beatbeatbeatbeatbeat* and my hormones would *popopopopop*. I would fill up with emotion so fast that if I wasn't in a constant state of expression about this love there was a chance the fullness would cause my brain to explode. And an explosion would be unacceptable because it would keep me from the pinnacle of achievement for a lanky, gangly junior high girl—finally becoming a high school girl who is equally lanky and gangly, but finally has breasts and a caboodle of her own makeup.

I would doodle about my love on any and every available surface. On a page of a telephone book. On the back of my hand. On the list of chores I had to do that day. I would tell my mom about how this boy was so cute, how I was certain he'd smiled at me when I was riding my bike casually around the neighborhood and happened to pass his house—twenty-two times.

The object of my affection was blond and tan with blue eyes that could lasso the heart of any young Texas girl raised to pine for the all-American Southern boy. This kid had "soon-to-be-star-football-quarterback" written all over his forehead.

Unfortunately for my aspirations of soon-to-be-girlfriend-of-star-football-quarterback, I wasn't the only one to notice him.

That summer, every girl I knew kept one eye focused on this young stud; I was far from the only one with a crush. All of them had his name scratched on scraps of paper in their rooms, each had imagined getting on the bus the first day of the next school year to find that he had saved a seat for no one but her. The cement on the street outside that guy's house was probably worn to deep divets for all the bikes that came to a sudden, halting stop in front.

A sudden need to tie the shoe!

To refix the ponytail!

I was not alone in my early tendency toward stalking, and I know this because that summer there were many late-night slumber parties when my friends and I would gather sleeping bags in our living rooms and all admit to being hot and bothered for the neighborhood heartthrob. Of course, none of us were bothered by the fact that our crushes were on the same boy. The point wasn't to win the competition, not yet at least. In those early days of crushes and love, the main goal was to know that you weren't floating in the sea of adolescent longing alone. And so we were satisfied by whispers into the late hours about this saint dwelling in our pocket of suburbia, this king of the cul-de-sac.

When the middle of July rolled around, my mother casually started to mention that Camp Grandma was approaching. She was likely counting down the days until her house would be silent, but for the first time in my life I was dreading the arrival. Going all the way to East Texas at a time like this? When there were day-to-day updates on who was playing basketball with my crush in the street, and speculation on whether or not the rumors were true.

The hot topic of the moment was that he was *experienced*. Everyone had heard the same rumor—which undoubtedly came from completely unverifiable and unreliable sources—that he had kissed a girl in his old neighborhood. We agonized over the possibility that this kiss might have included tongue-to-tongue contact.

I conferred with my friends, and it was decided that I absolutely could not go. No way, no how. And so without consulting my mom I picked up the phone to call my grandma.

She answered as she always did, by saying, "This is Grandma."

"Hi Grandma, it's me," I said.

She predictably wanted to know how I was and if I had been playing outside with my friends that day. She reported that the golf cart had picked up a nail in the neighborhood and was operating with three and a half tires.

"Yep, yep," I said whenever there was space in her story. Then, as soon as there was a sufficiently long pause, I launched into painstaking description of the problem I was facing. That spending a week away would be too long this year. I was getting older and all my friends were here, together, and I would be there, alone.

Grandma was quiet after my announcement. For her, silence is enough of an oddity that you always note when it occurs.

Now that I am older, I can imagine the blow this phone call delivered her. The granddaughter, who used to get more excited to see her grandma than anyone else in the world, was starting to look elsewhere in the world for happiness. Likely, she saw it as the end of a kind of innocence and the start of wanting more.

More than Slushees.

More than family.

More than what my grandmother could guarantee to provide.

Surely she was sad, but if any woman is a fighter, it's my grandma. She didn't stay married to a golf-playing, beer-drinking

East Texan for the better part of her adult life without learning the power of a perfectly played guilt trip.

She sighed into the phone, and commented that it was a shame, considering all the fudge she'd already made. And did she mention that she had enough spaghetti ingredients to feed a small army for a week? She knew exactly how to bait a pasta-obsessed girl like myself.

I might have been swayed, but I was standing my ground.

The Dairy Queen was always one town over, too, she reminded me. We could get Blizzards every day. (My family is much more than a group of people bonded together by shared DNA. We are also brought together by the ability to beg, bribe, barter, bait, and console using food. A lifetime of living in this family has created an interesting (read: fucked up) relationship with what goes in my mouth. To me, a piece of pecan pie is much more than butter, nuts, and crust. It is every Christmas morning that I mentally tabulated the estimated cost of my gifts versus my brother's and realized that the total amount spent on me was less.)

When I didn't immediately jump at the first offers of fudge, spaghetti, or Dairy Queen, my grandma likely knew it was time to pull out the biggest gun in her artillery. The trump card. The chip she had never thrown before. She likely knew she may never get an opportunity to win with it again.

"Did you know that I record every *As the World Turns* and *Young and the Restless* and that I keep them on tapes in the living room?"

Did I know? *Did I know?* Of course I knew. Those tapes were the forbidden porn of my youth, the temptation of my summers. How many times had I eyed those tapes and wished for the courage to ask if I could watch them, yet backed away for fear of being rejected by the one person in the world who had yet to tell me No.

I was speechless. Was she really offering me a window from the bubble of my life into the adult world?

"Of course," she continued, "if you were to come here and watch those tapes, well, there would be no reason to ever mention that to your mother. We all know her opinion on soap operas." Here, she interjected a (not so) casual yawn. "But what she doesn't know can't make her mad, now can it?"

My mother had enforced the no soap opera rule after I came home from school explaining that all my friends watched soap operas with their mothers, and why couldn't she and I do that, too? For a junior high girl who feels like she is on watch for being left out of a group from when she wakes up in the morning to the moment she puts on pimple cream and goes back to sleep at night, this rule set off a red alert. Actually being on the sidelines of an activity—any activity—had been known to encourage behavior ranging from obsessive smelling of one's own breath to a steady diet of nothing but air and Chris Isaak in the walkman. My mother consoled my loss by reminding me that not every family was alike. Other families might watch soap operas, but we didn't. No family was better than another for the choices they made, everyone was just different.

My junior high brain translated: *Different* meant complete and utter social outcast.

I begged. I pleaded. I explained that the entire time at lunch that day I had to smile and nod and make sure that I always had a chicken nugget in my mouth so no one could ask me why I wasn't adding to the soap opera conversation. I chewed and chewed until every nugget disintegrated into strings of soggy, moist dental floss in my mouth.

But my mother would not be deterred. Much like the no rap music and no *Wizard of Oz* rules that had dropped like wet blankets onto the vitality of my youth, this rule was sticking—for now at least. Any repercussions to the caliber of my coolness be damned.

Now my beloved grandma was offering a loophole in the law, a way for me to tiptoe over the line without feeling bad for crossing it.

I could do right by the rules of my mother and not lose face with my friends.

I could spend a week of Camp Grandma mercilessly studying a hitherto unexplored world in the television ether.

The catfights!

The intrigue!

The outfits!

The makeup!

For the first time in months, the neighborhood heartthrob fell from my mind and I told my grandma that she was right, what my mother didn't know wouldn't hurt her. Then I announced that I was more excited than ever to attend Camp Grandma that year, and wouldshepretttyplease make sure to remember she had promised a daily Dairy Queen Blizzard as part of the scheduled activities.

She assured me that she would not forget, and we settled on an arrival date. I hung up the phone, hormones *popopopopoping* at the thought of the secret viewings to come.

When the week of Camp Grandma finally arrived, my expectations were met and exceeded. There was an avalanche of food that would put two inches on my hips just for thinking of it today. Ice cream mixed with peanut butter cups and a steady stream of spaghetti. We turned the upstairs living room into ground zero of Camp Grandma. At anytime of the week you could find two cups full of iced tea, a bowl of candy bars for snacking, and she and I wrapped in blankets while we watched soap opera drama unfold in front of our eyes.

My grandfather took semipermanent residence in the room with the pool table, the closest room to the main exit of the house.

This allowed him easy departure for the golf course any time noises that could be construed as semiorgasmic floated from the soap operathon upstairs.

For a girl whose sexual experimentation had peaked at practicing French-kissing on the back of her hand, that week represented a learning curve in my sexuality that has yet to be beaten and could probably only be matched by the week that followed my first vibrator purchase.

I saw men and women jumping in and out of each other's beds, stripping down in offices, lying for sex, stealing sex from other people's spouses, finding their happy place from sex. Until that week I thought sex was something to be embarrassed about and hidden, tucked into the margins of sex ed books where it would be safe from the world of slamming doors, big hair, and even bigger emotions. The women in these soap operas were not like women I had seen before. Their lives were glamorous and powerful, and they wore clothes I was certain I'd never seen at JCPenney.

When I said that I was fairly certain they were the most beautiful women in the world, my grandma jumped to warn that moving to a big city and trying to be glamorous would result in nothing but the kind of heartache I saw on the soap operas. Why not stay in Texas forever—or even better than Texas, why not stay at Camp Grandma—until I was old and gray?

But her warnings didn't break through. That week was the first time I realized that maybe, just maybe, I wanted to become the kind of woman who was beautiful and alluring. The kind of woman who made men want to peddle *their* bikes to see.

Now that I am an adult, I've discovered that plenty of women pop straight from the womb into the world with their self-knowledge and sexuality intact. These are the women who have innate knowledge of how to catch a man's eye and smile at the right time, as well as which box of hair dye will produce the shade that always manages to sparkle, even under the dingy lights of a dive bar. Those battles have, unfortunately, always been hard-learned for me.

The only thing more pointless than the money I spend on vodka tonics are the twenty-dollar bills I throw at my hairdresser every month—after an unfortunate misuse of Sun-In that took a year to grow out, I know better than to take highlights into my own hands. Learning how to smile seductively is a skill I still haven't quite mastered, and I do manage to catch a man's eye now and then, but not always for reasons I prefer. (It's not that I get falling-down drunk, it's that I get drunk while wearing high heels and then fall down.)

That week of soap operaholism was when the switch flipped *on* in my brain. Maybe, just maybe, there was value in spending time to poof the bangs that had spent the better part of my life flattened against my forehead. Perhaps the self-imposed school uniform of oxford shirts (preferred by overzealous hand-raisers everywhere) weren't doing much to generate extracurricular attention.

Maybe these sentiments would have occurred to me but would have never been followed through on—perhaps I would still be wearing an oxford button-down and producing more right answers today—if it weren't for the phone call I received on my last night at Camp Grandma.

I had given my grandmother's phone number to my best friend in the neighborhood, along with specific instructions that she use it only in case of extreme emergencies. When she asked for elaboration on the definition of extreme emergency, I had my answer ready: hurricanes, fires, cancellation of school for the upcoming year, and any monumental updates on the king of the cul-de-sac.

My grandmother and I were sitting in the living room when the phone rang. We were both surprised by the shrill sound—no one ever called her house after dinnertime. She gave me a look that suggested either someone was seriously injured or my mother had used her superhuman parenting powers to intuit that her daughter had been receiving sexual education via soap operas—in which case I might be seriously injured soon.

My grandmother answered the phone and then handed it off to me. That's when I knew something must be very, very wrong. Only one person had this number. And that person was under strict instructions not to use it unless absolutely necessary.

"What happened?" I asked my best friend. One tiny part of me hoped for a hoax, but as soon as I heard my friend sigh into the phone I knew the call was no joke.

"It's all over," she said.

"What? What? What?" I asked, rapid-fire. I stretched the cord of my grandma's phone into the kitchen so I could spread my body on the cool tile floor. Even as an adult I believe it prudent to lie down when bad news is coming. Then, regardless of how hard the bad news knocks you, there's no worry of pesky details like balance. All your attention can be focused on whether you are going to deal immediately with the bad news, or get really drunk first, deal with your hangover, and then deal with the bad news.

There was no hurricane approaching, no wind or rain that would bring imminent death and destruction. We were going to continue with our regularly scheduled school year. But the news my best friend delivered still rocked my personal universe: The king of the cul-de-sac had chosen a queen. They had been spotted canoodling at the country club pool. And it wasn't light canoodling—it was serious for suburbia. His hands applied sunscreen on her back, lingered underneath the back of her bikini top, and then reached around her neck so he could kiss the side of her cheek. There was no chance the details got confused on the climb up the gossip chain, the entire affair had been witnessed firsthand by my best friend. An entire summer of devotion, lost to a no-named female who was wearing a bikini at the pool while I was camped out on Grandma's couch.

For the first time in my life, heartache leaned its full weight into my chest. From the whine in the voice on the other end of the line, I knew I wasn't the only one suffering. At home, a legion of junior high girls were bemoaning the loss, a defeat worsened because it arrived as the sun was setting on our beloved summer.

I told my friend I would see her as soon as I returned home the next day and we hung up the phone. I continued to lie on the floor. I tried to picture this girl who had won the gold medal of summer. In an instant, a person who probably looked just as awkward as every other girl on the brink of adolescence morphed—in my mind—to one of the beauty queens of the soap operas. I pictured her as a lynx who didn't need the padding to fill out her bikini top. The kind of girl who entered modeling contests for *Seventeen* magazine and was actually considered for the cover page.

My grandmother yelled from the living room to ask me what my friend had said.

"Nothing," I yelled back.

I didn't think I wanted to say anything, but then thought better of it. If saying nothing felt this awful, I'd have to say something.

"I'm never going to have a boyfriend," I shouted. Never was not an exaggeration. I was absolutely positive that I would spend the next eighty years alone. Then I would die. And then be buried alone.

"That's not the worst thing in the world," my grandma yelled back.

I picked myself off the floor and walked into her bathroom. I stood in front of the mirror, imagining changes that might make me into the kind of girl whom boys wanted to rub suntan lotion on.

One eye was oval, the other almond. If only they were the same shape. The freckles on the bridge of my nose, I was sure, were bigger than any other freckles I'd ever seen—a smattering of thumbprints instead of the cute dots that sat on other girls' noses. But there was little I could do about any of those things, not then, not before I had a bank account I could use for as much plastic surgery as I pleased.

I resigned myself to the fate of starting another school year as the same old awkward me who had ended the school year before. But then I looked down, and the idea arrived. I *could* take my attractiveness into my own hands: I could simply take the hair off my legs.

The light blond fur covering my legs could be removed in an instant. It would be so easy, and I would automatically look so much older and more mature.

My mother had never said no, I couldn't shave my legs. Not directly. (Even though I was fairly positive I had never directly asked.) But I didn't let that concern stop me. I was lit up by more than hormones. A conviction had begun to blaze in my soul that if I wanted to take a step into womanhood, the leg I put forward should be silky and smooth.

My grandpa's razor was in a shaving cup shaped like a German beer stein. I took it out and then pushed my hands on the counter so that I could shove my whole body on top of it.

Before I could stop long enough to think something rational like, "This isn't how women shave their legs in commercials on television," or even, "Perhaps I should think twice before taking a sharp object to my skin," I splashed water on the bottom of my right calf and then dragged the razor from my ankle to my knee. I had sloughed off about half the blond hair on my right calf when my grandma showed up at the bathroom door.

"I'd ask you what it is you are doing but it's pretty obvious," she said.

"Is it supposed to hurt like this?" I asked. My leg was fire ants. Acid. Fireworks popping in every pore.

I followed her eyes to where the skin on my leg was bubbling up with tiny red bumps.

"Well," she replied, "I might have advised you to use soap. Maybe some shaving cream."

These solutions were coming a little too late. Everything hurt—my leg, my exaggerated teenage heart.

I did not continue to shave my legs. Instead I put the razor down and let the slow burn on my skin heat into a raging fire.

My grandmother took a towel, wet it with hot water, and then wrapped it around my leg. Then she dried me off and helped me out of the sink. I hung my head so that she would not see the tears puddling in the bottom of my eyes. I had thought that if I could get that smooth skin, the kind of skin boys liked to rub suntan lotion on, that it would be a victory. (Perhaps this seems like an illogical train of thought, but logic becomes relative when you consider I've grown into a woman who thinks a tax return is free money the government *intends* for you to spend on shoes.)

Instead of telling me I had made a mistake, my grandma took my hand and walked me to the kitchen. Then she sat me in my regular chair while she got to work.

Because of that night, I am unable to think of chocolate chip cookies with whipped cream and ice cream as just triangles of chocolate, butter, flour, and dairy products of varying consistency. To me a chocolate chip delight tastes like a temporary fix for your heart when your love chooses another. It tastes like a calm place to sit while the world, as you know it, is spinning out of control.

It was a decade and a half later when I found myself in desperate need of my regular chair in my grandma's kitchen. But I was eight states away from Texas, so instead of taking a seat and resting my head on the cool countertop, I did a lot of aimless walking in search of a comfort I could not yet name.

I was living in New York at the time, so it was easy to pretend that this walking had purpose. Sure, I was walking *somewhere*, say, to the grocery store. But I was living in Brooklyn and the grocery store I was in the mood to go to would be in Union Square. I decided to forgo the subway and walk across the bridge, meandering up the city streets until I was in the center of New York, fighting my way into the store amidst strangers toting bags filled with cereal boxes and cheese wedges. I shopped, then took my bag back across the bridge and unpacked it in my kitchen. I could spend entire Saturdays this way. Walking to random museums, bars, apartments of friends, places I could stay long enough to look at a couple paintings, have one beer or say hello, and then duck out again.

My mind also did its fair share of wandering during this time; I was forgetting a fair amount of things. How to stand with my shoulders square with confidence instead of shrugging forward. How to go to the gym on a regular basis. How to stop at the second glass of wine instead of drinking the entire bottle. How to think *I forgive him,* instead of *I hate that bastard,* when considering the man who had broken up with me and left the apartment we shared a few months earlier.

I had a job I was spending far too much time at. But I welcomed the distraction. And there was a group of girlfriends who were my floaties in the baby pool of despair I was bobbing in. We would gather in small bars at late hours, when our workdays were finally done. One of us after another would straggle in, all of us huddling around small tables with overpriced drinks. After all, *this was the dream* and hell if we weren't living it. The too-small cubicles, too-small apartments, and skirts that were, unfortunately, a little too small since our lifestyle left us little time to do much but work, drink, eat. Not even my walks were much help for my waistline, as I tended to punctuate them with trips to various cupcake purveyors located around the city.

At first I wondered how I had ended up living in New York City alone. Then I would remember each move, the decisions that had made so much sense at the time. Leaving after college

JUST DON'T CALL ME MA'AM

graduation to work a big city advertising job in Boston. Moving with the man I loved to Seattle, then crossing the country again so we could take a chance on the Big Apple. Friends from Texas would call and ask how I was doing after the breakup. I'd answer my cell phone from the discomfort of my cubicle or while I was crossing a city street and I would assure everyone I was doing fine, just fine.

On a day when I wanted to convince myself of that, I might say that I was doing great.

Were there men in my life, they wanted to know.

Of course there were! Oodles of them!

There were men who came through my office building to freelance in graphic design or television production. They wore sleeves of tattoos and discontented expressions and I would fall in love with them for the day, the week, or if their projects were extended, the month.

One might ask me where the copier was and I would answer with a flush. I became a master of mentally extending meaningless conversations to a date over wine and tapas, possibly a vacation to the Bahamas and then the inevitable wedding, tastefully small, in the Berkshires. Which my imaginary love and I would follow up by life in a hippie commune, taking our art out of the corporate world and into a more pot-smoking, flower-loving, *organic* habitat.

I would return to certain city blocks where I had spotted a good-looking man crossing the street. I routinely visited the same Starbucks, the one with the hot, young barista I was sure could be the Ashton Kutcher to my inner Demi Moore.

The mental bubble I was living in was growing bigger and bigger, threatening to stretch out so far that no one would ever be able to reach in and shake some sense into me. The job, the friends, the imaginary relationships that could never hurt me because, um, they weren't real. All of it was adding up to a life not lived. But if I ever got close to realizing that this sad state was my current state of affairs, I would simply add an errand to my to-do list and start walking, or find a work project to wrap my brain around into the wee hours of the night.

"What do you think about getting a Brazilian?" my best friend asked me. We were huddled around a high table in a dark bar, sipping sangria with two other women. I was mentally contemplating whether I wanted to elevate the night to a martini affair or simply stay with the light-drunkenness of alcohol-saturated fruit.

Clearly my mind was not in the game, so to speak. I reminded her that Latin men weren't usually attracted to me. Something about the small waist, curvy hips those men were known to like did not jive with my figure. I specialized in hips that were round, but not exactly curvy. And unless I sucked in, I could feel my stomach hanging over the button of my jeans.

No, no, I was sure that a Brazilian man would definitely be out of my league.

When I looked up from sucking the wine out of an orange, I saw that all three women at the table were staring at me as though I had just said I was thinking of switching careers and becoming a trapeze artist. Or that I was contemplating giving up birth control because hey, maybe being a single mom living in a six-floor walkup in Manhattan would be *fun*.

"No," my best friend said slowly, "A Brazilian *wax*," she enunciated with exaggeration, giving me an opportunity to say ha-ha, of course I know that a Brazilian is a type of waxing that removes every single hair from your genital area, and, as an added bonus, from the inside of your bum, too.

But I didn't say that. I was a Neanderthal who'd been hiding in the cave of a long-distance relationship land, located outside the wide world of waxing. Fancy bikini waxes were for some other woman's life. The woman who woke up and roared at the day, who chewed men for breakfast and then spit them out for lunch, who didn't occasionally find herself standing in the produce section at the grocery store for long periods of time, unable to recall what was already in the refrigerator at home.

Not to mention that getting a Brazilian wax would mean that I had every intention of someone actually seeing the result of that wax, instead of just imagining that someone would.

"Aren't those waxes kind of, um, painful?"

The table was losing interest with my naiveté. Each of the women reached into their wallets. At first I thought we were calling it a night and getting the check, but instead of producing credit cards each of them pulled out a business card with the same name and phone number printed on it. The name was Lena, and the address was buried in an anonymous block of midtown.

"Compared to what you've been through lately," my best friend said as she threw a card in my direction, "this should be a piece of cake."

I took the cards, but I still wasn't sold on the idea of exposing my nether region to a complete stranger. The properly prudish Southern girl in me might have been buried under layers of cynical cement ala the city of New York (and broken dreams), but she was still in there. Somewhere.

"Don't look so freaking gloomy," my best friend advised. "You'll love it, you can *take a walk* to get there."

I wondered if my floaties were starting to deflate, and if this was the moment my friends were telling me to *fucking just swim* already.

And so I booked an appointment and a week later I found myself standing on that anonymous block in Midtown, giving myself a pep talk to open the door, step inside, and announce myself.

"I am Anna," I could say. "I am here to *roar*."

Two men were standing on the sidewalk to my right, smoking cigarettes with a ferocity that implied they were waiting to get to the end of the current cigarette so that they could light up the next. They had the look of men who were exhausted with the day

CALL ME AN ADVENTURER

before it even started. Like tax accountants in the throes of late March.

I contemplated walking away from the salon, continuing with my day as though the appointment had never been made. I wondered if one of the smoking men could be my soul mate if I were to meet him in, say, April. Timing, they say, is everything. With that thought, I took a deep breath, opened the salon door, and stepped inside.

A woman was sitting at the front desk. She was twirling a piece of hair and staring at her cell phone. I forgot my intent to roar.

"I'm Anna?" I quietly suggested. Perhaps she didn't have me in the books? Maybe Lena had called in sick today? Could my best intentions be rewarded by me being released back into the world of nameless men and cigarettes, city blocks to stumble by, boxes of cereal awaiting me in my kitchen?

The woman looked up at me from the books. "Brazilian with Lena." She said.

I nodded my head.

"Take a seat, she'll be out in a minute." She went back to her cell phone.

The verdict was in: I would not be saved.

To my left was a floral sofa—the kind that makes a grungy garage sale complete. A selection of magazines were fanned out on the table in front of the sofa. Articles on how a little Kama Sutra every day could keep divorce lawyers away. Ten steps to shed pounds from your body. How to change your life in just thirty days. For the better! And the betterment of all mankind!

I sunk in the sofa and ignored the suggested self-help.

I tapped my foot.

I started to get nervous.

After all, I wasn't completely convinced that removing hair was going to peal away much more than, well, a layer of hair. If I really thought stripping away layers would leave anything more than

JUST DON'T CALL ME MA'AM

the same ole me standing in the same ole spot maybe I would have signed up for therapy, or at the very least a yoga class.

I had motivated myself to get a job and an apartment and every semblance of the single-girl life I was living because the single women I knew who had jobs and friends and independent lives were happy in a way I never saw when I was growing up. I figured that if I just did what they did then eventually I wouldn't be sad about my break-up or confused about the future. If I followed their lead I wouldn't just be smiling on the outside. A Brazilian would be just another box I checked, thankyouverymuch, as evidence to everyone that I was living. I may not be a master of cause and effect scenarios—it took me weeks to understand that my ex coming home late with alcohol on his breath while promising through his teeth that he had been working late meant trouble for the relationship. But I do know enough to understand odds are good that when hot wax comes into contact with your genital area, the genital area will scream.

The pain, I tried to convince myself, would simply be the proof that I was alive. Like my dad always said, it's easier to move a car when it's started instead of when it's standing still.

"Zou Anna?" a voice asked from the back of the room. I snapped to attention.

"Yes?" I answered. Declarative sentences, they were escaping me that day.

The person waved me back, and so I stood, gathering my personal items and looking one last time at the covers of the magazines. Shedding pounds might have been a better answer, I thought. If extreme pain was about to come my way, it was my fault. I'd cracked the door, invited the pain in. Hell, I'd practically pulled up a chair so it could get nice and comfy.

"Iz very nice to meet you," Lena said once I reached where she was standing. I could not place the accent, but it seemed Eastern European. My world history was a tad foggy, but I thought I

CALL ME AN ADVENTURER

recollected a long and storied history of sadistic pain delivery in that part of the world.

Her hair was bleached blond and pulled back from her face in a tight bun. I was wearing high heels, but she still stood half a foot taller than me. And when she shook my hand, her palm covered mine like plastic wrap covering a muffin.

"Go to room five and take off everything below your belly button," she said. "No panties," she added.

Luckily, I wasn't so far out of fashion that I wore panties that reached above my belly button, but I saved the sarcasm. I wasn't sure it would translate.

I stepped inside the room and started to close the door. Typical procedure in salons I usually frequented was that you got a moment of privacy to undress and get situated on the table. But Lena did not waste moments. The door hadn't shut before she stepped in behind me. So much for the illusion that *anything* would be left private.

I stood in the far corner while she washed her hands. Slowly, very slowly, I stepped out of my jeans.

"No panties," she said again, without turning around. I was not moving quickly enough for her. I took a deep breath and dropped my drawers. The last thing I needed was to piss off the woman controlling a cauldron of boiling wax two centimeters away from the part of my body I depended on for sexual satisfaction.

"Here I go," I said as I climbed aboard the table. "All ready now. Yep, I'm ready. Ready as I've ever been."

I chatter when I get nervous. Which is why I pity people who have to sit next to me on long plane flights. When there's bad weather. And the plane won't stop rocking. And the flight attendant did not stock her fridge with enough miniature bottles of wine to keep me calm.

I laid my head back and for the first time in my life—without a doctor's office gown to provide cover—presented my full frontal to the world. No soft lighting. No soft pillow to cry into if Lena announced that what I'd shown was not quite up to snuff.

"I do ze left side, ze right, zen center and back," she said. She was testing the consistency of the wax, pulling a Popsicle stick up and out of the smoking substance. She cooked her wax in a container that was a close cousin to the Crock-pot. I thought of my grandma then, and her love of Crock-pots. I thought about what she would say if I told her I was getting a Brazilian. The last time I visited her, she had insisted on doing my laundry and she had taken a break to ponder the purpose of my G-strings when she was transferring my clothes from the washer to the dryer.

"Doesn't look like it does the job underwear is s'posed to do—one little strap can't keep much from jiggling. And it sure as heck doesn't seem like it would *be* comfortable," she observed. I had replied that very little about being a woman was turning out to be comfortable. Then my grandma put the underwear in the dryer and mumbled something about those words going from my mouth straight to God's ear.

"Iz your first time, no?" Lena asked. She was holding the first application of wax in the air.

"Um, well," I stuttered. "I've been waxed before," I said. I couldn't help but watch the stick of wax. It was like knowing your elementary school teacher was about to slap your hands with a ruler and all you could do was watch the ruler come closer and closer until it finally hit your skin. You knew it was going to hurt like hell, but still you couldn't look away.

"Waxed, yez. But never taken *all* off," Lena clarified. Her tone implied that lesser waxes were the training wheels to the bike ride, the gas station merlot to its more complex cousin.

She wiped the wax from a spot on my left hipbone to the inside of my thigh. If you picture the left side of my abdomen as a rainbow, this first piece of hair removal would be like erasing red and orange from the sky.

"You want to leave strip?" she asked me. Her hands pointed to the inch of hair that was centered on my exposed vagina.

"I don't know," I said. "What do you think?"

"I zink that most people know whether they like a ztrip or not."

Subtract a hundred pounds and exchange the waxy Popsicle stick for a *Cosmopolitan* and Lena could have been my mother. Neither woman had patience when I waffled.

"Let's take it all off," I decided. "After all, this could be the only time I get this done."

"No," she said with a smile. "You will come back for more. They alwayz come back for more. They alwayz come back to Lena."

She refilled her stick with more wax, and then turned back with a flourish.

"All off!" she exclaimed.

I gripped the side of the table with surprise at the vigor she showed to the application. We were no longer moving slowly through the colors of the rainbow, and before I could voice any apprehension, she had covered the remaining front hair with wax. Yellow. Green. Blue. Purple. The heat was close—very, very close. These temperatures could melt Styrofoam, I didn't want to consider what they could do to my clitoris.

"All off is okay, isn't it, Lena? It's, um, not going to injure me down there?" For some reason saying the word vagina was proving difficult, even though I was showing almost all of it. My maturity level was reverting the more nervous I became. Pretty soon I was going to start giggling, and referring to it as my private parts, or maybe in a reversion to toddlerhood, my pee-pee.

Lena positioned her hands over the large strip of wax that was now ready to be removed. I could tell she was positioning herself for one hell of a pull. "Only two women go to the hospital with Lena. And one was for up here"—her finger drew an imaginary circle around her right temple, communicating the universal sign for crazy—"not down here."

Then she yanked so fast it took my voice a minute to catch up with my scream.

Lena didn't skip a beat. And like a good toddler, when no one paid attention to me, I quieted my scream to a whimper. The surface of my skin was red with blood and anger, but this did not stop Lena. She stretched the pores and plucked the few hairs that had survived her pull.

"You very good for this kind of wax," she said. "Hair iz removed clean, no break. Very, very good."

I felt like I had just swam through a sea of jellyfish and she wanted to discuss the most irrelevant parts of the journey—like the consistency of my freestyle stroke or how well my bathing suit coordinated with the welts all over my body.

"Lena," I said, then I cleared my throat. "Why did the second girl go to the hospital?"

She was preparing wax on the stick again. Always with this woman, more wax. As though it were her job. As though I was paying her to do this to me.

Oh, right. I was.

"She was not a very smart woman," she said. "I told her not to move, and instead she jumped. I told her very, very loudly, no move. But she did. And poof!"

"Poof," I repeated.

"Poof!" she said. And then, "Ready zoo continue?"

I briefly considered the feasibility of convincing a man that half-finished Brazilian bikini waxes were the new style. Like when mullets came back in fashion for a minute, and even though every-one with half a brain and no Arkansas blood suspected it to be a very, very bad trend, no one spoke up until a legion of hipsters had adopted the style and it was too late to turn back. The half-wax could be the trend I passed off as cool, even though deep down I would be rooting for it to grow back very, very fast.

She pulled the front folds of skin apart and wiped a layer of wax inside. Until that very moment in time, I did not know that part of my body grew hair.

"Hold thiz back," she said. "And now iz the very, very important time for you to no move."

She didn't have to tell me twice. "No move," I said. "No poof."

"Good girl," Lena said. And then she patted the top of my head. I held the two flaps of skin back, like they were Batwoman wings with the power to fly me up and out of this crazy cave I had found myself in. My pride was now officially in the trash with the other used pieces of wax.

Lena reached in and gave one a pull, and then the other. This time I did not scream, or even yell. I thought happy thoughts. Nothing so happy that it was unrealistic—like lying on the beach in Jamaica. The thought of not leaving the salon in an ambulance was happy enough for the moment.

"Now for your backside," Lena said. And when I looked at her for confirmation, visually asking her to repeat what she had said so that I wouldn't make one of the more embarrassing mistakes of my lifetime and present her my bum when she hadn't really asked for it, Lena graciously elaborated.

"Doggy style," she instructed. She must have had her doubts that I would find my way without direction because then she contorted her body into a triangle so I could see what she had in mind.

My pain threshold was worn so low I couldn't even appreciate that I had entered an alternate reality where directions were given via sexual positions. It almost seemed *normal* that my esthetician had just demonstrated doggy style.

"Right," I said, "doggy style."

I was in the home stretch figuratively, and also literally, and so I balanced on my hands and knees, and separated my kneecaps a foot apart. One little drop of sweat fell from my forehead between my hands and I focused my attention on that. It was easier to look there than to know a virtual stranger was examining the more intimate angles of my backside.

She waxed and pulled, and when she was finished, she tapped me on my shoulder.

"Finished," she said. As though removing hair from back there was as normal as, say, starting the day with coffee.

I laid down flat on the table and took a breath. All that intimate exposure of my body and not even an orgasm to show for it.

Lena was bustling around the room, throwing away applicators and straightening up her machine.

I stared at the whitewash wall, catching my breath. A picture flashed into my mind. Me, with a more sophisticated backdrop to my life. Me, as a woman so glamorous she'd faint before saying the words "doggy style" to anyone. Me, as the woman I dreamed I would grow into. When did I veer off path of becoming that woman? From this vantage point—me laid out on a table with a burning crotch and an empty apartment waiting at home—it seemed more likely for me to be a cat lady than a lady with infinite power of seduction.

"Zou have a date? A boyfriend you get first Brazilian for?" Lena asked.

Probably a question she asked most clients. And even though I probably wasn't the only client to have a pitiable response, I felt utterly alone as I answered her.

"No date," I said. "No boyfriend."

I continued to stare at the wall.

I turned my head to face her and thought about sitting up, until I remembered that I still had no pants on. Logically, I knew modesty was a moot point. But it seemed more appropriate to show a full frontal when work was being done to the frontal area in question. Now that the job was completed, my timidity had returned.

Lena walked around the table and looked at me. She cocked her head in curiosity. I'm not sure what she saw in my expression, but a realization seemed to dawn on her.

"Up, up," she said. And she motioned for me to stand.

I sat up on the table and gathered the towel on the table to cover me.

She put a hand on my back and nudged me further. I pushed off the table, towel still in place, and stood on my own two feet.

She turned around to the sink to wash her hands, and I took the opportunity to step into my jeans. One foot, then the other. I regretted not having worn a skirt, or maybe sweatpants. Anything but denim that already felt restrictive against this new freedom.

She dried her hands and then turned to face me. Once I was finally done situating myself I looked up and realized she had been watching me.

"Pain here," she said, and she took one hand off my shoulder to tap on my hip, "will go away in one hour, two maybe. No extra work from you, it just goes away."

"Yes," I agreed. My plan was to leave her salon and march straight into a store where I would buy a bag of frozen broccoli, take it home, and sit it in my lap until the burning stopped. Very little work from me. And the only waste would be one partially defrosted bag of florets.

"But," Lena continued, "tat iz not true for every pain."

Then she raised her hand up and touched my chest. "This pain, you must work very, very hard to make disappear."

Then she patted me on my head and walked to the door. Before she left, she advised me to be back in three weeks. "Not a day more than zree weeks," she reiterated.

— 44 —

I told her that I would see her then and when the door closed I sat down on the chair.

Outside the streets would be teeming with people. People who had their lives together, people who knew what they wanted, people who made a conscious decision not to sink.

I had two choices.

I could join those people in the streets.

Or I could retreat.

It would be easy enough for me to sink back into the comfort of the South. People would be there to comfort me. People would understand. It's okay to go home with your tail between your legs when you've been dumped. I could spend the next two weeks on my grandmother's couch watching stories about lives more glamorous than the one mine turned into.

The bubble I'd been building around me was just the distance I needed to be able to walk away with no strings attached. But there, in the silence of that little white room, through the screaming of my burning skin, I heard my answer: I did not want to walk away.

I did not want to wander aimlessly.

I did not want to mimic the people around me in the hopes that looking normal would finally feel normal.

I did not want to love imaginary people.

I wanted to find a way to love myself. In the least Chicken-Soup-for-the-Soul-way possible. If that was possible for a heart laden in cynical cement.

I would pay the receptionist, I decided. Then I would walk out into the day and bum a cigarette from one of the men who would probably still be smoking on the street. I would consider asking what he was planning to do next April, but then I would remind myself that I needed to focus on what could happen *now*. So I would simply thank him and then turn away.

I would smoke that cigarette while I walked to the nearest store, where I would purchase frozen broccoli, chocolate chip cookies, whipped cream, and ice cream.

I wasn't going to swim today, but I sure as hell wasn't going to sink. The plan was to stay afloat until I'd done enough work to fix the only pain that really mattered. Not what was burning on the outside, the rip had opened my insides.

I had not learned my lesson the first time it was taught to me, back when I had my grandmother to help me lick my wounds. But I would take the tools she had shown me for survival and repurpose them for the circumstances I was standing in. And I would learn my lesson, oh would I. The mistakes of pouring your heart into an imaginary love and all your dreams into imaginary glamour would not be made a third time.

Chapter 3

Call Me a Lady-in-Waiting

In the dream there are two choices.

One, Freddy Krueger. Waiting in a dark alley with his finger-daggers of destruction and I've got nothing but a bucket of extra-buttery popcorn. There is nowhere to run and nowhere to hide. My only solace is to bury my face in the vat of airy, light kernels and hope that he will pass by and leave me to live another day. My heart races. Butter is everywhere, in my nose, dripping down my face. I hear a girl scream. I scream. I wake up, heart pounding.

Two, I participate in a wedding.

In the dream at least there is the chance I could go the way of the undead with Monsieur Krueger. But awake I only have one choice. I slip on the taffeta, apply lip gloss, and prepare for my march down the aisle, hoping that lady luck is on my side.

Hating weddings is about as un-ladylike as a lady can get in our times. Hell, in most people's book it's more than just un-ladylike—it's downright un-American. A wedding that a girl can't afford to pay for is practically an unalienable right. Like freedom of speech and freedom of religion, the freedom to pick an over-priced dress and costume your best friends like jelly beans (even though they'll all secretly confide that *you* are the first bride to, like, ever pick the perfect pink for a bridesmaid dress) is a rite of passage that any female baptized in popular culture expects to exercise in her lifetime.

But I hate them. Oil and water. Armadillos and road. The guts in the pit of my belly wrap into a nervous fist when it comes to being a part of a wedding. I once discussed this issue with a psy-chologist. Before I terminated our sessions because the co-pay was cutting into my sushi budget, we were able to deduce two causes for my wedding phobia.

The first is what's commonly known (in my immediate fam-ily at least) as The Amy Grant Extravaganza. This might be the first time you've ever heard of the singer/songwriter Amy Grant. Don't feel bad—that just means you spent the '80s listening to Madonna and Michael Jackson with the rest of the pre-teens in America. If you'd had the pleasure of growing up in the Bible Belt and attending an ultra-conservative private school, you'd know Amy Grant better than the back of your hand. (We knew the back of our hands well, mind you, because those hands spent many hours locked together for fervent prayer.)

Eventually Amy went mainstream, but to us private school preadolescents, her glory days were when she was giving glory to God. If you'd given me the choice between Amy Grant or my very favorite multi-colored ink push out pen, I would have committed to write in black ink for the rest of my life. That Amy Grant, she was the bomb diggity bomb. In less parochial terms, one might call her *the shit*.

My awe of Amy Grant's awesomeness was how it came to pass that for my talent show in the third grade I lip-synced one of her songs.

Oh yes, I did say lip-sync.

Karaoke is what drunk people do in bars. Lip-syncing is a talent that is the sole domain of platinum-selling artists like Britney Spears, and third graders everywhere. I practiced more on that song than I had for anything in my academic career to that point. Phonics homework? Screw that—there was a talent show to win. I'd honor my mother and father, but I'd be darned if I wasn't going to *crush* the competition.

I learned all the words, even memorizing when to take my breaths and swallow so that my throat bobbed as though I was actually singing. When I finally took the stage I felt as though I was channeling the Christian pop princess herself. Unfortunately, the sound crew at my elementary school wasn't channeling the roadies employed by Ms. Grant. About thirty seconds into my *song—snap, crackle, pop, pop*—and the sound went dead. Silent. Quiet from the speakers. But the song was still playing in my head and so I kept lip-syncing: "Angels watching over me every move I make."

Finally, the moment arrived. When I finally heard the silence. I dropped my head down to face the audience and realized I no longer had Amy to hide behind. I was standing, alone, on stage, the focal point for the attention of the crowd. I panicked, and my little elementary school girl brain made a bargain with the God she prayed to every morning when she woke up and every night when she went to bed: If He would help her get out of this alive, she would never, ever put herself in front of a crowd so she could accidentally humiliate herself like this again.

I did get out of it alive, but I'll ask you this: Do you know how many moments there are to humiliate yourself as you walk down the aisle? *Do you?*

The second reason I believe I have wedding phobia is what has become commonly known (in my extended family) as the Flower Girl Flop. My dear Aunt Fran was married when I was but a wee little thing. Four and a half years old, about as tall as an adult's knee, with blonde bangs I preferred to wear in my eyes so that I could hide at a moment's notice. You might have thought me maladjusted, but I lean toward the friendlier and more gentle term, "loner."

Fran thought I would be darling as a flower girl. My mother claims now that she had her concerns, but in the end yielded to her sister because, after all, who doesn't want to see her child excel in challenging new situations. They dressed me up in a precious gown and then gave me a basket of flower petals. The petals, I was told, were to be distributed as I slowly walked up the aisle. They would tell me when to start walking and when I reached the preacher I was supposed to stop.

I remember standing at the back of the aisle, looking at everyone's backs. *This won't be so hard,* I told myself. All I have to do is walk and drop, walk and drop. What I didn't anticipate was that all those people sitting in the seats would actually turn around to watch me. I heard the music change tempo at the moment my mom gave me a nudge and told me it was time to walk. I took one step and every single one of those faces turned to watch me step and all I could think was *drop.* So I did. I dropped every one of those petals in a pile right at the start of the wedding march. And then I ran. As fast as I could. All the way up to where the preacher was standing. I was sure that if I could reach him then I could go back to being invisible, my duty would be done.

Again I ask, Do you know how many moments there are to humiliate yourself as you walk down the aisle? I sure as hell do.

This is why every time a friend gets engaged I make sure that I pause to have a moment of sheer happiness for her. Because I know that soon, very soon, the panic will set in. Soon, very soon, the call will be coming. She won't be calling to find out what's new in my life, or to ask if I've had time to check out the sixty-two photos of her engagement ring that she emailed around. This friend will want to know if I will be one of her bridesmaids. I've answered that call enough times to know with 100 percent, absolute, positive certainty it should be avoided at all costs. Because once I pick up the phone, I end up saying yes, and then the madness begins.

It's nothing against my friends who have gotten married. Most of them are extremely nice people with, ahem, fabulous fashion sense, who would never dream of dressing their bridesmaids in colors normally reserved for mermaid costumes.

And it's nothing against what weddings symbolize—I believe matrimony is a beautiful thing. It's just that it's even more beautiful when I am simply attending the ceremony and not participating. Because really, is there anything better than spending a Saturday night in the middle of *someone else's* family drama? Raising a glass to the happy couple, the stoned younger brother of the bride, the overbearing mother of the groom—it's like being a fly on the wall of someone else's Thanksgiving Day pain, but with better food and a band. When you're simply a guest, you come and go as you please. A little ceremony here, maybe twenty minutes of the reception there, some cake, and a Houdini out the side door.

As a Southern girl, there are things I am naturally supposed to be good at. Cooking pies, for example. And sitting through college football games with a smile on my face and my date's bourbon flask in my purse. I am supposed to remember to wear slips underneath summer dresses and panty hose to any occasion that will also be attended by a Southern lady over the age of sixty.

Those things I understand.

Those things I can bumble my way through with some fake piecrusts and a couple emergency trips to the lingerie store.

There is still hope that one day I might master those things.

But when people expect me to know the one thing that should come most naturally to a Southern girl—how to be a lady-in-waiting to her bride—that's when I start to shake like a porcupine and search for the nearest exit.

My difficulty with being a bridesmaid is similar to the trouble I have balancing myself on skis, reading the business section of the newspaper, and sticking with a job for longer than two years: Even after all these years and all this practice, I'm still just not very good at it. Maybe it's the childhood trauma, maybe it's me—but it hasn't been easy to find my sea legs for standing by the bride's side.

First of all, I don't cry at appropriate times. And that doesn't make for a very good bridesmaid. These crying inconsistencies aren't going anywhere; they've been a problem my whole life. I could be in a hospital bed inches away from my death, receive news that marijuana just got legalized so I am going to miss out on all the fun, and also discover that my puppy was killed in a freak hit-and-run accident with a tandem bicycle, and still I wouldn't be able to shed a tear. But then if the nurse brought me red Jell-O instead of green, there would be no stopping the waterworks.

As a bridesmaid, chances are I will cry when the catering staff closes up the appetizer buffet instead of when the bride says "I do." That's the cue for all the Southern blue-haired ladies to cluck and point and speculate that I am one of *those* girls all screwed up in the head because she's always a bridesmaid and never a bride.

So there's the tears—and then there's the bridesmaid march. Every time a wedding planner explains that the bridesmaids have to walk down the aisle in rhythm with the orchestra, I picture myself bouncing like the main character in a Mentos commercial and my mind starts to freak out faster than an unmarried sixteen-year-old peeing on a stick. The sound speeds up in my head, I have a flashback to the Flower Girl Flop, and it's all I can do to keep from *running* to my spot at the altar. Inevitably, by the end of the night some good ole boy who's had too much scotch finds me at the reception to comment that I woulda been real purdy in the ceremony if I'd slowed down 'nuff for anyone to take a gander at me.

Good ole boy buddies of the groom, drunk on scotch. Yeah, I'm not so good with them either.

The last thing I'll bring up—which I realize exposes my extremely selfish nature and innate desire to be the subject of (most) every sentence—is my inability to understand why bridesmaids take the proverbial back seat in the friendship *for the entire* engagement period. Let's say I have a life crisis. Let's just say, for instance, my manicurist moves back to Vietnam. I call my friend, the bride-to-be, expecting a sympathetic ear. Instead I get an earful about the latest wedding crisis—the preacher is double-booked and can't perform her ceremony, etc, etc.

Now I know for a fact that you can't spit in Texas without hitting one of eight million churches, all fully staffed with men (and occasionally women) of the cloth. Yet there is no sympathy for the fact that the one woman who could do my nails without destroying my cuticles is gone for good.

Ye'sirree, I can fake an orgasm with the best of 'em, but when it's time for me to fake excitement about being a bridesmaid, I fall flatter than a perm on a hot summer day.

And so instead of answering the call, I typically let it go straight to voicemail, and then spend at least twenty-four hours stewing about my fate. In a bar. With a glass of vodka, and maybe a side of soda. Because I know the moment the bride asks me to be a bridesmaid and I say yes, I will be destined to spend the next year involved in the worst kind of relationship, the relationship almost guaranteed to fail, the relationship that seems perfect right until the devastating end—the long-distance bride and bridesmaid relationship.

Being a bridesmaid has always been a long-distance affair for me because each of my friends who has gotten married is from Texas, and so all of them had their ceremonies in that great Lone Star state.

Since I left Texas about 2.2 seconds after graduating from college, I've always been a plane ride away from all the engagement parties, bridal showers, and actual ceremonies. The brides have been very understanding about the distance, and happily allow me to substitute phone bills for the expense of flying down for all 316 functions celebrating their pending unions. Which is all well and good until I fly to Texas for the ceremony, arrive at the first event, and realize that I've been relying on the distance to keep me sane.

As the long-distance bridesmaid, I spend all kinds of time talking to the bride about her planning, and how much I am looking forward to finally being there in person. She's happy with my performance. I start to think that maybe, finally, I've figured out the whole wedding thing. By the time I show up for the celebratory weekend I'm as high as a kid who's been sucking helium, thinking I'm the ultimate, invincible bridesmaid who can do no wrong. But it only takes minutes of actually being in the same zip code as the wedding for my balloon to pop, and for me to remember, yet again, that the next time I see a bride-to-be's number pop up on my phone, it's better to pretend I am on a month-long camping trip in Cambodia with no phone reception than to act like I'm woman enough for the bridesmaid job.

I may look like a twentysomething female of full mental capacity who should be able to function in the role. But deep down I'm still the four-year-old hiding behind her bangs. I'm still the frozen third-grader onstage, mid lip-sync, wondering if I am going to make it through the evening alive.

I was a bridesmaid for the first time eight years ago. The bride was a close friend from high school and throughout college, even though it was becoming evident that our lives would be going down very different paths. Her path was neat, clean, and lined with beds of flowers—comparable to a pleasant road in the Netherlands. Mine leaned more toward a back alley in Amsterdam. But we still shared a lot of history, and my excitement for her nuptials was genuine. I thought I would fly from my home in Boston to Texas and slide into the role of bridesmaid like a dainty little hand into the quilted comfort of a cooking mitt. Instead, when I got out of my rental car at the bridesmaid luncheon, I found I'd reached for the hot plate without any protection at all.

Welts.

Burns.

Arugula salads.

Cucumber sandwiches.

Overwhelming questions I couldn't answer about *"how my life was going"* and *"wasn't it great that everyone was starting to get married"* and *"when I asked how your life was going, I meant to ask if you would be getting married anytime soon."*

And that was in the first fifteen minutes.

The bride-to-be, who used to love afternoons with beer, enchiladas, and flip-flops air-kissed my cheeks before excitedly showing me the collection of Cuisinart appliances she'd already received. I had initially thought the "his" and "her" vibrators in my suitcase would make a good gag gift, but I could see they would remain

CALL ME A LADY-IN-WAITING

packed away until the holiday season, when my office had their annual White Elephant party.

I had never met this side of the bride. And if I wasn't familiar with this part of her personality, was I really cut out to stand at the altar as one of her closest friends? Not to mention, was I really expected to go into a store and purchase an appliance that could be used for a purpose other than sexual satisfaction? Clearly this whole bridesmaid situation went way outside my area of expertise. It was borderline emergency. I needed wisdom. At the very least, I needed suggestions on how to sneak some vodka into my cucumber sandwich.

I only knew one person capable of giving me both, and so I called my mother.

My mother loves nothing more than to give advice. She's okay on giving out recipes, and doesn't really mind giving birthday gifts. But what she really loves to give is advice. She considers it her God-given duty to stamp an opinion on as many people as possible while she's on this earth. Sort of a modern-day Dear Abby version of a rancher who would brand the ass of any cow that happened to linger too long in front of her.

"This bridesmaid thing isn't what I expected," I whispered into my cell phone.

She wanted to know why.

"Well," I said, "I don't have any of the right answers to the questions people are asking me."

"And?"

"And I don't have the first clue why a blender needs more than three speeds."

"And?" she asked. Apparently the things that were sending me into a tailspin weren't even raising her sails.

"They want me to eat cucumber sandwiches," I complained.

I'm a vegetarian. I should have loved that a cucumber sandwich was anywhere near my plate. Usually in Texas you have to peal back half the ass of a cow to reach anything green. And even then, the green is most likely just the color of the ceramic. But to me, eating a cucumber sandwich is like asking someone about the weather—you've managed to take up space, but not to add any sustenance.

"You've survived worse," my mom said.

I didn't think that I had. "Did I mention that all they have to drink is iced tea?" I asked.

She didn't say anything for a moment. If there is one thing in this world that the woman loves more than a Cosmopolitan, it's a dramatic pause.

"Do you remember the summer I signed you up for Vacation Bible School and every morning you would cry and tell me that I was the worst mother in the world? All because I was trying to shower you in the love of Jesus?"

I did.

"Do you remember when your father forced you to sign up for the 4-H group and everyone made fun of you because you didn't know how to milk a cow? But he made you go until those girls threatened to beat you up because you were on the drill team?"

I did.

"You survived all of that," she said.

"But not without permanent, painful scars," I pointed out.

She accused me of ignoring the silver lining. Because of those experiences I knew enough Bible stories to at least make a passable argument for myself at the gates of Heaven. And I also knew how to shovel manure.

"Perhaps you just need to find the silver lining about being a bridesmaid," she suggested.

I sat there for a second, pondering the idea. It sounded a lot like trying to look on the bright side. My parents had been telling me that for decades, and I so knew from experience: Positive thinking can be a total pain in the ass.

"Wait!" she said. "Don't all your friends get platinum rings these days? You should be looking for the platinum lining."

"It's easier for me to love you when you don't imply that I'll never have my own platinum ring," I said.

She said she understood.

I understood what she was saying, too. And so began my bridesmaid odyssey across Texas. I would finally be adult enough to stop hiding behind my bangs and try to conquer my fear of crowds. Inside every cucumber sandwich, bedazzled on every pair of bridesmaid shoes, behind every look of fake rapture, I would search for the platinum lining.

I've learned to grin. To bear it. And not to freak out and cry when the wedding planner asks me to walk to the beat of the harpsichord. Instead, I wait to cry until I am in the bathroom. When, for no logical reason whatsoever, the sound of running water reminds me that somewhere, a baby seal is dying.

Platinum Lining #1: Being a bridesmaid in a Texas wedding is a little like being a groupie for a famous rock band.

Twenty-nine years of living and I'm finally ready to admit it: I'm just not that cool. I'm a fairly nice person with good hygiene and a list of charities I donate to during the holidays. But when God was giving out membership cards to the cool kids club, I must have been in the bathroom powdering my nose, because being hip has never come naturally to me.

I started to accept my lack of coolness when I lived in New York City and was surrounded by people who were truly cool. These were the people you read about in magazines—who get photographed on the street for their style and set the trends the rest of us will follow. These are the people who discover the next big indie band at a small dive bar in Brooklyn. They have a few beers with the band, convince the band to change their style, up the tempo, and—*boom*—the band gets big, and the cool people get a permanent backstage pass.

I've always enjoyed music, but I usually arrive on the scene long after the trendsetters have departed, and so my interest is maintained from a distance—as in the distance from the cheap seats to the stage in a megastadium. I've never been invited into an entourage. I've never basked in the glow of fame. And now that I've passed the cute, perky age of those girls that rock musicians like to pluck from the crowd, I must come to terms with the fact that I will never be a groupie.

In lieu of that experience, I will settle for my time as a Texas bridesmaid. There are lights. There is music. A high level of ego-maintenance is required. And also all the Evian water you can drink.

Musicians spend their entire lives working toward their pinnacle performance, perhaps at Madison Square Garden or maybe headlining a music festival with Tom Petty or some other I'm-a-big-name-rock-star in need of a career boost. This is exactly how a Texas girl prepares for her wedding. First you learn to crawl, then to walk, and next you learn to walk down the aisle. After a lifetime of preparation, it's understandable that by the time the big day arrives, the Texas bride expects all eyes to be on her. And like a rock star demands a perfect environment backstage before the performance, it is the bridesmaid's job to keep the bride calm before she presents herself to the crowd.

And so I know the rush of adrenaline a rock musician feels when he walks onstage because I have seen that same look reflected in the face of many a bride. And I can imagine how great it must be for the groupies who get to hang out with the rockers, because I know the deep satisfaction that comes when the most important person of the night taps you as the special helper—even if it is only to help her raise the layers of her wedding dress so she can properly sit on a toilet.

CALL ME A LADY-IN-WAITING

I may never party in the penthouse of the Four Seasons with international music sensations, happy just to be breathing their recycled carbon dioxide. But damnit if I haven't gotten all the taffeta a woman could ever dream of, and made the most of every eye that (accidentally) connected with mine as it wandered toward the main attraction walking a few feet behind me.

Platinum Lining #2: I do not take food for granted because I know the pain of starvation.

I became a vegetarian after I left Texas. When I'd go back to visit and explain my vegetarianism, people would respond in ways that confused me. Comments like, "Yes, but you eat chicken, right?" and, "But surely you aren't a vegetarian on Thanksgiving," indicated it might take a while for my friends and family to grasp the concept of my not eating meat.

I thought that eventually people would come around. Besides the argument that "animals have feelings, too," there is also the fact that they have eyes and hearts and oftentimes children, and, well, it just didn't seem like such an outlandish thought that a person might have a problem eating them.

I thought wrong.

As a bridesmaid, I assumed the "Beef or Chicken" reply card that came with my invitation didn't apply to me. Surely spending $700 on a plane ticket, dress, and gift—not to mention being a good friend of the bride—meant someone could ask the kitchen to put some lettuce on a plate, maybe spice it up with tomato and salad dressing.

I thought wrong.

I was once en route to a chapel and had a bride call me on my cell phone to remind me I should pick up something to eat because there would be no food for me at the wedding. She suggested a jack-in-the-box that was on the way. I chuckled, "Ha, ha . . . ha?"

I thought—no, I hoped—she was joking. Partly because it seemed ridiculous there would be no vegetarian option at the wedding. And partly because it was laughable that anyone thought jack-in-the-box served vegetarian fare.

But sure enough, when the beef or chicken plates were served, no element was salvageable for a vegetarian palate. Texans aren't Neanderthals. They read the food pyramids like everyone else. But right after they add a starchy mashed potato and a green vegetable to the plate, they start to worry the meat and poultry section is feeling neglected, so they cover the whole affair in a gravy with so many meat chunks you could put the cow back together again.

After drinking my dinner at the open bar and waking up the next day with a head that hurt even worse than the hunger in my belly, I learned my lesson. Now I know that when the waiters circle with appetizer trays during cocktail hour, I need to snag all the crackers I can get. I understand that every cheese square on a toothpick is a treasure to be cherished, and no martini olive should ever be left to waste.

Platinum Lining #3: If I didn't bring my low levels of estrogen to the party, nothing would get done around here.

In 2003 I packed my luggage and left for vacation. I spent that vacation on a beach in Miami, but my luggage headed to Germany, without me. It must have been quite a life-changing journey, because that luggage decided never to return home. I can respect that sometimes vacations change us in monumental ways. For example, when I was in Miami I discovered the joy of a piña colada for breakfast and have never turned back.

Even though I thought I lost that luggage a few years back, even now I will find myself wondering what happened to a certain sundress, or looking for a CD I suddenly yearn to hear—and I'll realize those items were packed in the luggage that disappeared.

I believe my estrogen must have been packed in that luggage, too, because it was around the time I lost that luggage that I noticed myself acting differently than other women I know. They had rounded a corner where they discovered domestication and diamond rings were fulfilling. Like I said, I was busy getting filled up on piña coladas.

And that lost estrogen has yet to find its way home. When a cute kid walks through the door, I think, *A very short person just entered the room,* while every other woman gravitates to said short person like a shopper on a day-after-Thanksgiving sale.

It used to be, when all of us bridesmaids would gather around the bride during the preceremony female-bonding time, and other bridesmaids would coo over pictures of someone's baby, or ask me when I planned to get married, I would get tongue-tied and urgently start rifling through my mental chest-of-drawers for the proper answer. But instead of finding the words I was supposed to say—"Soon! Just as soon as I find My Prince Charming!"—all I could do was wonder what set me so far apart from my friends. Could I blame it all on estrogen? Or was there something more psychological at play here?

But I have since learned to use my speechlessness for good instead of awkwardness. I know I have nothing to say in those conversations, so I look for tasks to keep me occupied. I refill glasses of champagne while the other bridesmaids gossip with the bride. I check in with the wedding planner so we will know how much time remains before we need to line up at the chapel door. I organize bobby pins and lipstick bottles. And as long as my champagne glass stays full of piña colada, everyone wins.

Platinum Lining #4: If I'd never been a bridesmaid, I never would have realized that being in a sorority really did teach me a life skill applicable in the real world.

The sorority house wasn't all pillow fights and late-night Ouija board sessions. We had serious, character-building moments as well. Like when one girl would decide she wanted to date another girl's boyfriend, and so the nasty rumors would begin. Was she really sneaking out of the sorority house at night to cheat on him? Had she actually put on five pounds in the hips or was that just a bad pair of jeans? Believe you me, it only takes a few trips through the rumor mill to learn the difference between friend and frenemy—when you can let your guard down and when you need thick skin.

And so when a wedding photographer is asking you to turn to your "good" side, or a rather insensitive wedding planner decides you are the only bridesmaid who won't get a seat at the official bridesmaid table because the other bridesmaids all have dates and there's no room for the odd-numbered single girl, you think back to the days of the sorority house and thank the good Lord that you paid all that money so you could be part of the club. Otherwise, you might never have learned that not every slap has to be the beginning of a catfight—for some people, slaps are just second nature.

Platinum Lining #5: Sometimes being second best is the best way to be.

Every Texas wedding I've ever been to has included six or more bridesmaids. One wedding had twelve. It's reasonable to assume six to twelve bodies can get the job done, and that a bridal party should not have so many people it could double as a flag football team.

But Texas wasn't a state founded on reason, it formed because of a group of men who wanted the world to operate by their rules, damnit, and they were going to stand in a fort and shoot people until anyone who didn't agree with them was dead.

In a state where many people go to state schools, and those schools have sororities with hundreds of members, whittling down nearest and dearest friends to a list of ten names is a difficult task. Add in the sister of the groom who, unfortunately, has to be a bridesmaid because the bride is, like, totally going to have to spend every holiday with her for the rest of their lives—and the shortage of spots at the altar becomes nothing less than a full-blown crisis.

At some point in the last couple decades, a Texas bride decided to take matters into her own hands and simply write a new wedding rule that would solve this crisis. In addition to choosing a bridal party, she would also choose a house party. This group of house party girls would not be as special as the bridesmaids, but they would be more important than other women who were invited to the wedding. A middle tier, per se.

To show their specialness, members of the house party would sit in the second row of the church, right behind family members of the bride. But so the bridesmaids would still know they were the most special of all, the house party girls would simply wear a black dress they already owned, and wouldn't have the privilege of purchasing an over-priced, pseudo-ball gown they'd only wear once in their lifetimes.

The first time I was invited to be in a house party, I was like, "What the hell?" I mean, I'd been a good friend to this bride—I thought I'd been a good enough friend to earn the bridesmaid role, not a seat in second place. I'd held back her hair while she puked up party punch at a fraternity party. I'd let her cry on my shoulder when she flunked her take-home children's literature final exam and I even waited until she had left the room to crumble in a ball of hysterics at her inability to pass a class that fraternity pledges were known to sleep through and still pass. Not to mention, it was a *take-home* exam.

Sure, I'd accidentally burned a hole in one of her cashmere sweaters with a cigarette. But that was at a New Year's Eve party, and the whole damn theme of the New Year's holiday is to let bygones be bygones.

But I accepted my house party designation, ironed my black dress, and got ready to be a back-up player. And what I discovered about being in the house party is that it's so much better than being a bridesmaid. It's more than just having your cupcake and eating it, too. It's having your cupcake, eating it, and then getting all those calories magically erased.

Being in the house party means you have been chosen as an important person, but that importance has no responsibility attached because there are already bridesmaids running all the errands for the bride.

You don't have to march down the aisle by yourself because girls in the house party walk in twos.

You don't have to stand up during the wedding, which is a lifesaver when you've got a Southern Baptist preacher who wants to take a few—or forty—minutes of the ceremony to speak on the importance of fidelity.

And at the end of the show, you still get a ride on the special bus that takes the bridesmaids and groomsmen from the wedding site to the reception. You know what that means? If you're at a Southern wedding and you're worth your tequila salt then you do—free beer!

The Monday I returned to work after being a house party girl, I got to thinking about being second best. I wondered if my happiness at being in a house party could translate to more happiness in my office life. For so many years, I'd strived to be the bridesmaid of the office—the woman people looked to first. But the second-string players have a layer of people cushioning the blow from major explosions. If I stayed a couple steps back, I would still catch shrapnel now and again but I'd never be in the direct line of fire. I might even get to go a few weekends without a colleague calling, begging me to come in to the office for just a "couple" hours.

People know second-string players, and trust that they are good workers, but they don't look to them to solve the fire drills that keep corporate America up at night. I tested this theory and sure enough, it was true. Now I slack without actually being viewed as a slacker. And I owe this realization—that has become the beating heart of my corporate existence—to being a house party girl and learning that sometimes second best is the best way to be.

Platinum Lining #6: The open bar makes unacceptable actions sound acceptable. Don't listen, that's just the alcohol talking.

As a bridesmaid who suffers from stage fright, I know the general giddiness that can erupt at a wedding reception when the open bar opens for business. But I also know the pain of the morning after a conga line—oh yes, I do. What starts out as a tonic, far too often flares with a temper.

I've watched people who stayed away from the buffet line at dinner dive four slices deep in the wedding cake because their third gin and tonic gave them the go-ahead. I've seen dedicated couch potatoes take the advice of tequila and next thing you know they're doing the Macarena faster than you could have said TiVo. I've struggled to encourage bridesmaids from my own ranks to stay away from little brothers of the groom. Chardonnay may sound like a friend, I warn, but she's leading you to pain. Bridezilla is likely to make a special post-wedding appearance when she finds out one of her besties spent quality time in the parking lot with her new brother-in-law.

Decide not to drink so much alcohol that it speaks to you— problem solved. No voice in your ear wondering what it would feel like to request Tone Loc. The temptation for a quick dip in the hotel pool sans Sunday's finest? Completely removed.

I can't tell you how many times this lesson has saved me at an office party. Oh wait, yes I can. I still have my job so that means this lesson has benefitted me at each and every office party I've ever been to. Slowly now, back away from the sauce, and wake up tomorrow without regret.

Platinum Lining #7: Wedding speeches are moments we can pretend all our dreams really will come true.

The first time I went to a wedding and heard the speeches, I was overwhelmed by feelings of insufficiency. The people getting married were not just perfect for each other, they were also perfect in the eyes of the friends and family who stood up to speak. Full of fun times, forgiveness, and boundless friendship, the bride and groom were not capable of doing wrong. Here I was, a person who occasionally lost her temper with her family, cursed coworkers from her cubicle, and oftentimes woke up with a chip on her shoulder for no reason at all.

I looked under the table and wondered if there was room for me to curl into a ball of shame. Thank God I *didn't* have a date for this wedding. At that moment he'd likely be looking at me from the corner of his eye, realizing I was wildly insufficient.

But then I blinked a couple times and focused my vision on the bride and groom. I saw that they were people, human beings like the rest of us—and like the rest of us they probably hadn't lived perfect lives. That's when I realized what wedding speeches truly are: pockets of time when we get to press pause on reality and take a break from mind-numbing jobs and relentless mortgages—not to mention the crushing realization that we're all grown up and the window of being a famous athlete or a rap star has closed forever. Wedding speeches are the moments when people getting married can shine. And the speech-givers can enjoy the halo effect of that glow.

Because really, how often do we really get to praise the people in our lives? Maybe it's just me, but the last time I delivered a spontaneous compliment was 1992. As long as you aren't worried about telling the whole truth and nothing but the truth, wedding speeches can be a time to boost the egos of people you care about. Which is so much more fulfilling than boosting the ego of your boss, or someone you think you'd like to take home for the night.

When you give a wedding speech, you can paint the picture of a life sans pimples, broken promises, or random bouts of prostitution. You can be like a walking, talking greeting card that's all rainbows and sunny days, ladling out bowl after bowl of Chicken Soup for the Soul.

I have no idea what it's like to be married, but conversations I have with married people suggest it's not an easy venture. Why not give the bride and groom one last night to believe they have found the only flawless person on earth, before they have to wake up the next day with rings on their fingers and morning breath blowing on their faces?

Platinum Lining #8: Not all men are heartless, insensitive bastards.

I hate the word Feminazi. And not just because it suggests there is a point where feminists cross with the most horrific people to ever walk the planet. I hate the word because every time I make a comment that puts males into one large, easily bashable group, that word lights up in my brain and starts flashing really bright. Then I have to wonder if I am, in fact, being Feminazi-ish. And as soon as I wonder that, I have to slap my own hand for using a word that suggests there is a point where feminists cross with the most horrific people to ever walk the planet.

The problem is that sometimes males *need* to be put in one large, easily bashable group. Because sometimes a girl deserves a good vent. And if you are a girl who is frustrated because she just went on her fifth bad blind date in as many weeks, there is not one distinguishable target for your frustration—it's the whole, large, easily bashable group of them.

I was in just this state of mind when I attended a wedding last year. Because I was a bridesmaid, I was invited to the rehearsal dinner that took place the night before the ceremony. It was a lovely, well-decorated affair that actually offered vegetarian dining options. If I hadn't been so busy avoiding every man in the room because I was convinced the whole lot of their species were total imbeciles, then I might actually have been enjoying myself.

The speeches began after dessert was served. The groom's buddies stood up and told stories; I shot all of them looks of death. I saw through their drunk stories and hardy-har-har jokes; underneath those chuckles were men who wanted to destroy everything good in the world. Bunnies, unicorns, the hearts of sensitive and caring women *like me*.

Then I stood up and said some words about the bride and how great she was, how wonderful female friendship was—while managing to avoid elaboration on the hypothesis taking shape in my brain that the world could have been an exercise in peace, hope, and understanding *if* females had been the only ones walking the planet. I hadn't quite worked out the whole procreation part of the puzzle, but I was sure the solution was out there somewhere.

But then the groom stood up. And as he started to talk about how he had spent his whole life looking for the woman he was going to marry the next day, I felt the iceberg in my heart start to melt just a touch. Sure, we all know he was exaggerating the situation. I was a sixteen-year-old girl once who knew plenty of sixteen-year-old boys. A boy at the tender age of sixteen isn't dreaming

CALL ME A LADY-IN-WAITING

of his future wife, he is dreaming of finding a woman—any woman—
who will loan him use of her breasts.

But when the groom stood up and said those words, I realized
that we are all just out there doing our best to relate to people.
Sometimes the connections work, sometimes they don't. But just
because I've had five connections fizzle in a row doesn't mean I
have to spend the night throwing forkfuls of tiramisu at anyone
with a penis. Not *every* man is a heartless, insensitive bastard, just
the ones I was lucky enough to date.

If that's not a platinum lining, I don't know what is.

Platinum Lining #9: When you think everyone is looking at you, no one is.

I always think I am being watched. Always. At home, I will not
walk in front of a window naked. No matter that there are mini-
blinds on the window. And curtains. And a layer of shrubs separating the window from the outside. There might be someone
watching! With binoculars! That see through walls!

Add that to my stage fright issues, you've got yourself a
woman who can't walk into a room without feeling like eyes are
following her around. And this isn't arrogant in a Paris Hilton
I-am-so-awesome-people-*can't-help*-but-watch-my-every-move.
It's much more I-have-to-check-my-shoe-every-two-minutes-to-
make-sure-I-am-not-dragging-toilet-paper-around. The opposite
of arrogance—it is actually a plea for non-attention.

This has always been my own personal challenge as a bridesmaid. It's hard to be the wallflower you want to wilt into when
your job description reads "must remain calm and collected when
the attention of the congregation turns your way" with the addendum of "while wearing a brightly colored dress that crinkles every
time you take a step."

But the fascinating thing I've learned is that for every time you
think the whole crowd saw that moment when you tripped over

your own two feet, or those five minutes when you started to swoon at the altar—yet another bridesmaid fallen victim to the Texas heat multiplied by the bright lights on stage—no one notices. And you know why that is? Because everyone else is too busy wondering how many people saw the moment they dozed off during the minister's work, or overheard them snapping at their spouse on the way into the church.

That's often hard for me to remember in the moments I slide on my bridesmaid dress and overapply blush to my cheeks. But for better or worse, I'm not the only one with stage fright and/or the fear of being discovered as having no idea what she's freaking doing. This lesson ought to serve me remarkably well. Especially the next time I'm running late and don't have time to find a robe before dashing in front of the window.

Platinum Lining #10: When you think no one is looking at you, everyone is.

If people act like they aren't paying any attention to you, they are actually watching your every move.

I always suspected this was true, but my suspicions weren't confirmed until I was a bridesmaid in a wedding where the groom's ex-girlfriend was in attendance for the entire weekend. She was at the rehearsal dinner. As well as the ceremony. And then "mysteriously" wandered away once the vows were solidified.

The general sentiment was that the ex-girlfriend was still hoping that the groom would realize sometime during the weekend that the ex was his true love, stop the proceedings, leave his fiancée, and return to the arms of his ex.

Unfortunately for the ex-girlfriend, life does not operate by the rules of a Julia Roberts movie.

The bride and groom got married as planned, and everyone else at the wedding worked very hard to avoid his ex. I never saw her speak to anyone, except for one of the groomsmen who clearly hoped he could exploit this poor woman's heartbreak. But even though people weren't speaking to her, they were talking about her, and monitoring her every move. Was she standing too close to the groom? Showing too much cleavage? Looking a little too teary-eyed? Where is she in the chapel? Is someone in position to block her during the 'Who does not think these two should be joined in holy matrimony' moment?

I learned a lot from this woman and the time she spent stalking her ex-lover's wedding. Now, when the voice in my head says, *Pick up the dollar on the street and take it for your own,* I look around, and even though I think no one is looking at me I know that actually means lots of people are watching. So I pick up the dollar and yell into the empty street, "I see you looking at me, I know you are out there, waiting for me to pick up this dollar!"

One way or another, being a bridesmaid was bound to turn me into a crazy woman. The mission has been completed.

It's hard for me to believe, but almost one year has passed since the last time I was a bridesmaid. And I imagine it will be another year (at least) before I am a bridesmaid again. The first batch of weddings were my friends who wanted to be married in their twenties. The next batch will be those who spent their twenties doing other things—whether that be pushing their careers, living in places far from home, or just learning to sit with their single selves until being alone no longer makes them curl up into the fetal position and wonder how the world could be such a cruel and lonely place. And if I'm the only single person who has ever felt this way, my apologies to all you rosy-cheeked, perfectly-adjusted people of the world.

This space between my bridesmaid duties has given me time to ponder the difference between those women who choose the prior route and those of us who choose the latter. I'm curious to see if my friends who get married next will approach the actual weddings differently, since they've invariably had a different approach to the dating world from being out there longer.

I suspect they will not.

The tradition and expectation that comes with being a bride transports women into a role that even those in its throes don't seem to understand or are able to control. Since I'm not a woman prone to dreaming of a big, white wedding, I guess I'll just reserve the right to use the time allotted to me as a Bridezilla on occasions completely unrelated to an actual wedding—like every Monday morning for the rest of my working life. While I'm at it, I might as well also reserve the right to simultaneously bitch about and enjoy my own wedding, much as I do for everyone else's ceremonies.

My mom suggested that by just taking the wedding events at face value, I wasn't seeing the value they could actually bring to my life. Now I understand I need to look deeper in every aspect of a wedding. A bride might say, "I need someone to pick me up from my house, drop me at my hair appointment, and then pick me up an hour and a half later," but what she's communicating is that she has so much change on her plate, the idea of changing highway lanes on her own is too much to bear.

It used to be that every time I thought about screening a call from a bride-to-be it was because I felt I was being asked to put my personal discomfort at fancy Southern soirees to the side so I could stand at her side. On center stage would be my own insecurities and emotional baggage—the fear of being caught in front of a crowd with no background music to guide me, and no idea what move I am supposed to make next. But now I know that when my friends hear me say "Yes" they know I am really saying, "Please spare me the pain of helping you pick out place settings. Let me be the bridesmaid who takes you out and gets you piss-drunk." Piss-drunk being a deeper version of drunk required in times of layoffs, breakups, and the realization that your mother-in-law kinda, sorta sucks.

I never expected it, but I will look forward to being a bridesmaid again. Because the ultimate platinum lining I've discovered is that being a part of these major life events for my friends is a chance for me to step to the side, out of my own personal spotlight. I don't have to be the most cynical girl in the room, I can simply be one of eight trusted friends who steps up when the bride asks me to. Everyone needs a vacation from themselves every once in a while—even if it is just to a reception hall deep in the heart of Texas.

Chapter 4

Call Me a Foodie

There are mornings when it takes me almost an hour to choose what I am going to wear for the day. I have been known to stand in the soda aisle contemplating Diet Coke versus Diet Dr Pepper for at least twenty minutes. And there are people on this planet who love me dearly, but have likely contemplated leaving me on the highway to hitchhike my way home because of the time it takes me to choose a snack at the convenience store. But ask me whether I want to move to a new city, or what kind of car I'd commit to pay off for the next five (hundred) years and I'd have an answer for you within minutes.

This isn't glib irresponsibility, oh no, it's just the fucked up way my brain works. The easy decisions are painstaking, and the most painful changes are decided in a moment.

For most people raised in the South, and especially Texas, giving up meat is not something to be taken lightly. We're talking about a state in which the majority of the residents would choose eating meat over remaining a part of the Union if given the option. So in keeping with my tendency to make big decisions on a whim, I decided to become a vegetarian one day pretty much out of the blue.

If there were noble intentions perhaps it would be easier for me to explain the decision-making process, but there were not. I wasn't swayed because of the positive impact vegetarianism can make on the world's food supply, or even something simple like kindness to animals. It had nothing to do with saving the world. I really just wanted to save myself from the freshman fifteen that had turned into a sophomore twenty, and so on and so on, and well, you can call my mother if you don't get the picture. I believe she's saving a shoebox of old photos in case the need for blackmail ever arises.

The road to my vegetarianism is not linear or coherent in any way, but it does have to do with my losing battle against those college pounds I put on. When I graduated from college, I stopped drinking out of fraternity kegs, which should have helped me get rid of at least one chin. But when I got to Boston I discovered a temptation *even more alluring* than watered-down beer chilled to chugging temperature (if you can believe that). My new love? Italian food.

Growing up in the South, you miss out on the Little Italys and the North Ends of bigger, more cosmopolitan cities. Growing up in the suburbs of the South, you think Olive Garden is pretty good shit. Mostly because you innately understand that it's a step up from the only other Italian food you've ever eaten: Chef

Boyardee. But then you visit a city like Boston and you realize that saying Olive Garden is Italian is like calling Velveeta cheese. Just because a food is cheap, served in mass, and has enough preservatives to survive Armageddon, doesn't mean it's good.

As soon as I realized how much I loved real Italian food, I tried all the Italian restaurants in Boston that I could reach by public transportation. Then I expanded my sights to other foods I'd never experienced. Real clam chowder, real bagels, I discovered the Irish are experts at much more than just Guinness and I fell hard for shepherd's pie. Fresh cannolis? Check. Cream sauce? Well, it is a special occasion. Oh, it's not a special occasion? What the hell, cream sauce, check. Every restaurant had a specialty to try and these specials were completely unrelated to the buffalo wings and burger specials at the Bennigan's of my youth.

On weekends, I'd go to restaurants on my own. This was how I managed to stay occupied on long weekends that were short on friends. Other places I ordered from late at night when I was still at the office, selecting from take-out menus stained with coffee drippings and grease.

And even though I was conscious of wanting to shed the weight from college, Boston was heaven for a girl who's mother preferred Taco Bell to cook the same burritos and tacos for dinner night after night, but otherwise would serve pot roast, pot roast, and hey, anybody in the mood for some leftover pot roast?

Once winter rolled around, the weak attempts I'd made at trying to occasionally eat healthy (mayonnaise on the side, at least *asking* for low-fat salad dressing) got buried under feet and feet of that godforsaken snow. Whatever food was closest to my reach was what I would put in my belly. Enough time had passed that my college weight settled into just being my weight. I began to recognize those rolls in the mirror as my arms. And stuffing them into winter sweaters suited me just fine.

But then summer rolled around and I realized it was time to take drastic measures. I would run a marathon. 26.2 miles. Four months of training. Fairly drastic, right? Right?

Wrong.

I might be the only woman of all time to actually put on weight from the moment she started training to the moment she crossed the finish line.

So then it was time for *really* drastic measures. With no other choices, I resolved myself to the D-word: I would have to diet. I'd resisted for so long because food should be something that you enjoy, not something you fear.

I'd seen women walk down the dieting road and never find their way back. They'd take a turn to low carb/high protein and for the rest of their lives feel that damn pang of guilt whenever they reach for the breadbasket. Or a blueberry muffin. Or a tortilla. For God's sake, what kind of life is that? Others choose the low-fat eating path and find themselves regaled to serving after serving of fro-yo, never able to indulge in a scoop of Blue Bell without wondering whether the Oreo chunks were going straight to their cellulite.

The dieting neighborhood is nothing like Mister Rogers Neighborhood. It is not warm. It is not cozy. It does not welcome you with colorful sweaters and promises of smiling puppets. But I was tired of feeling my thighs brush together. The daily stress of the battle against my waistband was breaking me down. I'd had enough of the emergency trips to Filene's Basement for a larger pair of jeans. Pretty soon my boss would figure out that I'd exceeded my limit of "last-minute" dentist appointments. The heavy winter jackets I'd hidden under since running my November marathon would come off soon and that would reveal to the world that all that time the cotton layers had been unnecessary— all the extra skin I was hanging onto was capable of generating all the warmth I needed.

I scoured the Internet and hit the bookstore. And jackpot! I was like an evangelical stumbling upon a prayer book in the pits of a New York subway—there was hope! So much hope! In thirty days I could be thin. In sixty days I could be a freakin' supermodel. The part of my brain that wanted to believe it could be this easy advised me to jump right in, but then another part of me hung back.

What would happen at the end of the thirty or sixty days? Would I be looking for another book? For the next quick fix? Would I feel a pang of guilt when I reached for the breadbasket? Because *someday* I would have to reach for it again—a woman cannot live on juicing alone.

I take that back. Some women can live on juicing alone. But those are also the women who enjoy the elliptical machine. Now I don't want those who exalt the elliptical to feel I am against them. I'm for happiness in all shapes and sizes, but when your arms get that sinewy, muscular look that screams "I spend four hours a day on my elliptical," then yeah, I pretty much have nothing in common with you.

Pretty soon I found myself at the bookstore lots of days after work waging an inner war over my dieting fate. One day I happened to look over and see a title that caught my eye. There were none of those sculpted abs on this cover, no perky fitness gurus screaming from the page. The spine of the book was simple, and when I pulled it from the shelf it actually seemed quite boring. No surprise, really, since the book was all about being a vegetarian. People will try to tell you that it can be exciting to eat tofu and vegetables, but I've been a vegetarian for eight(ish) years and I can tell you that those people are lying. Vegetarianism can be pleasurable and rewarding. But exciting it's not.

Instead of spending a full paycheck on the hardback diet books, I doled out just a few dollars for the paperback book on being a vegetarian. I thought at the very least it would give me a few days, maybe even a week, to put off the beginning of the D-word. I'd finish the book, hem and haw for a few days, and then guiltily drag myself back to the bookstore where I would then buy the books that would slowly take over my life and crush my spirit one resisted French fry at a time.

Little did I know the book I actually purchased would keep me a passenger on the french fry train. Once I started turning the pages, I found myself surprisingly interested in what it had to say. And not in an if-I-don't-do-what-they-say-my-thighs-will-brush-together-forever kind of way. It felt more like: maybe I'll just give vegetarianism a try for, you know, a couple days and see how it works out.

Those couple days turned into a couple weeks and then months. I learned that I could be full if I didn't have chicken in every salad and that having a full meal didn't require a full serving of animal. At first I was embarrassed to ask for vegetarian items, as if people would drop what they were doing to accuse me of ignoring the food pyramid and then file my name away as an offender of the surgeon general. But people weren't nearly as inflexible as I assumed they'd be. In my office, everyone took it in stride. My favorite take-out restaurants didn't flinch when I asked for substitutions on my favorite dishes. The whole thing turned out to be rather uneventful, in fact. I found that if I was able to be a little flexible on the fish issue (which, *I know*, doesn't make me a true vegetarian—go ahead PETA and stage a rally about it) then I didn't have to be that girl in a restaurant that was like, "Can I get this without the bacon and that without the gravy and can you run through the ingredients in your Caesar dressing and wait, wait, wait—before you walk away from the table can you swear on the Bible (or another religious item equally dangerous to lie in front of) that no animal death has taken place on or near the dish I am about to eat?"

No one wants to go to dinner with that girl. And I still didn't have a lot of friends. I needed people to want to go to dinner with me.

In fact, my transition to being a vegetarian was so quick and smooth that I completely underestimated the impact of the phone call I'd make to my mother to tell her I was now a vegetarian.

I was thinking support, a round of verbal hugs, perhaps a couple offers of gift certificates for vegetarian restaurants in the Boston area. Instead I got silence. Then the muffled noise of my mother covering up the mouthpiece on her cell phone. I lived with the woman long enough to know what it means when she covers the mouthpiece: She is repeating what I just told her to my father.

I interrupted her relay of information. "So, are you going to tell me what you think about me being a vegetarian, or just talk to Dad?"

I got a cough, then the clearing of her throat. "I think if giving up meat makes you happy then that's great, love."

Uh-huh. I waited. Surely more would come. After a beat, it did. "It just seems like a big change to make. And you've had a lot of other big changes lately."

Uh-huh. I waited again.

"Do you think there's a reason you chose to give up meat after you moved away from the South and all your family and friends?"

I thought about this, but could see no reason other than too many trips to Filene's Basement and a fortuitous trip to the bookstore.

"Hear me out," she said. "You moved to a new place, got your first job, and your dating life has been full of brand new challenges."

If not being able to understand half the men I met because of their Boston accents was considered a "challenge" then I agreed with her. But did she really think those changes correlated to how I chose to eat?

Apparently she did.

"Granted," she said, "you've never moved to a new city on your own and this is your first job. But your relationships with people and food have run parallel paths for a long time."

This was news to me. My love life had affected the way I treated food before? And vice versa? Wasn't I more aware than that? Wouldn't I realize if I had *control issues?*

I asked if she wanted to contribute anymore commentary that could be potentially damaging and she said she was finished. For that night, at least. We hung up and I thought about what she said. For, like, one second. And then I went back to my real life. Reflection was something I had every intention of doing. Later. I put it on the mental to-do list of things I really had no intention of doing anytime soon.

Years passed, and occasionally I would think back to that conversation with my mother. I'd think about the dance of food and relationships in my life and wonder if they were moving to the same tune or if one had taken the lead and the other was hanging back, not quite in step. I'd question if there was substance to her observation or if it was simply coincidence.

There had been other times in my life when my mother had pointed out something that should have been obvious, but I could not see. There were the ill-fated ballet lessons, when I was *sure* that I was destined to be a professional ballerina but would cry for two hours before going to class because I was already anticipating how badly my toes would hurt when I was done. Gently, my mother suggested that maybe, just maybe, I'd do better with a jazz class where I clicked my heels instead of balanced on toes.

And then there was that year of high school when my mom spent months peppering conversations with words on peer pressure and *just saying no,* and then, sure enough, the first night my friends and I went out with the older kids someone put a bottle of always-classy Boone's Farm in my hand *I just said yes* and next thing I knew my lips were semi-permanently stained blue—not just from the liquor going down but also from it coming back up five minutes later.

Mothers, they know things. If only we always knew enough to listen.

As my twenties were winding down, I finally reached a point where it made sense to pause. I realized it could be wise to learn from the ways food had influenced my relationships in the past, so that I could use that information for better times in the future. I had been willing to give up meat, but I would never give up food. There were times of famine on the relationship front, but I had hopes for more consistent abundance in the future.

My mother is a woman who will joke about many, many things. But as a woman, fine jewelry is not one of those things. And as a Southern woman, pearls are most definitely fine jewelry. I came to realize, in my own time, that her pointing out that food and relationships were intertwined was my mother's way of handing me a pearl of wisdom.

It was time I pay attention to what was being handed down.

Lesson: Every cook will pay attention to a fire. Smart cooks know that the smoke also has something to say.

Best Paired With: A slice of tira-mud-su and any kind of alcohol that will put out the flames.

I will never forget the birthday when the presents went from genderless toys, like bikes and swing sets, to more girl-appropriate gifts, like dolls and sparkly headbands.

I don't burn bras.

I understand the cultural necessity in acting like a lady. (On most occasions.)

I'm not going to blame any therapist costs on the fact that eventually I had to stop digging for dinosaur bones in my backyard and start playing house if I was going to have any female friends in my lifetime.

But it was confusing for my seven-year-old brain when I unwrapped that first birthday present and found the googly eyes of a doll staring back at me. I had expected a videogame, or perhaps a science kit that I could use to make things explode. It was like someone pulled a ripcord—in an instant I fell out of the tree I'd been climbing and hit the earth with a thud.

After the first doll came a second. But it was even worse than the googly-eyed creature because this doll was a Barbie. The only time I had ever seen Barbie dolls was when the neighborhood boys stole them from their sisters and made a plastic bonfire in the road. My Barbie doll came with things women of every age were supposed to want—a Corvette and a mansion. I didn't want a sportscar or a house with a winding staircase. I just wanted to be back on my bike pedaling up the street.

By the time I got through my presents that year, the room was an explosion of pink—pink wrapping paper, pink doll boxes, and pink rims around my eyes from crying. You'd have thought someone stole my slice of birthday cake with extra icing from off of my fork for all the tears I shed. But actually the tears were for the one thing I didn't get but wanted most: streamers for my bike handles.

And then, beneath the Pepto-explosion, my dad found one present I hadn't unwrapped yet.

He walked it over to me and I opened it slowly, carefully. I feared what I'd discover inside. Was it a Barbie mall where I'd have to drive Barbie in her Corvette so she could buy Barbie furniture for her Barbie mansion?

I had given up on my seventh year before it had even started.

Up until that moment, toys had been good things. I'd always wanted toys. Lots and lots of toys. But that was before I discovered the world had so many *pink* toys.

Before you jump to any conclusions that this story is going to turn out like *A Christmas Story* when Ralphie actually gets his Red Ryder BB gun, I'll spare you the hopes of a happy ending. I got the paper off the gift and had to turn it like a Rubik's Cube to figure out what was inside. They were not streamers for my handlebars. Instead it was a box with illustrations of an oven, and pictures of food.

"Is this my own kitchen?" I asked my mom.

"Well," she said, "it's part of a kitchen."

I was not well-versed in the different parts of our kitchen. When my mother cooked, I was usually outside playing. The quiches and briskets magically materialized—like when we drove through Taco Bell and my mom talked into the microphone and the next thing I knew there was a bean burrito in my hand.

"It's an Easy-Bake Oven," she said, and she bent over to point out illustrations on the box. The pictures advertised cookies and brownies I could bake without the help of any adults, which was good, because at that moment I hated all the adults in my life.

"Maybe if you like baking with this oven, you can start making things in the big kitchen," she said.

In the following days, when faced with lifeless dolls and the plastic spaces where those dolls lived, I turned to the one gift that at least rewarded curiosity.

If I put Barbie in her Corvette and pushed, then the car went somewhere. Zero surprises. But if I plopped a glob of dough onto a pan and slid it into my oven, I ended up with a solid piece of food that could, technically, be eaten.

I turned into a cooking monster. Very few things that I made were good, but I didn't let that stop me. I baked the hell out of the packets of batter and then I would find the most unsuspecting member of my family—most often my younger brother—and force that person to eat the brownie, cookie, or more organic choice of tira-mud-su.

I got so busy baking new creations that I started to bail out on the boys and their bike rides by choice. I was obsessed, and that Easy-Bake saw more action than a frat boy with a hundred bucks on his first night in Tijuana.

Even though no one in my life said "Enough with the brownies (because eventually someone's stomach could get hurt)," the oven finally spoke up for them. One afternoon, when I was waiting for my creations to harden into the guise of edibility, I heard a flicker, then a *pop,* and looked over to see the flash that was the death of that oven.

My mother was summoned.

My crying was comforted.

The oven was laid to rest in a trash receptacle.

With my oven gone, I wasn't sure what to play with. I could go back to riding around with the boys, but something was different now—I was different.

I was still certain that I didn't like Barbie, but I wasn't against playing with the Corvette from time to time. I didn't have such an awful time playing house with some of the girls in the neighborhood, either. The pink wrapping paper was long gone, but the Easy-Bake Oven had left its mark. Its lesson: Once you get a taste of cooking, it doesn't easily let go of you.

Fifteen years later, my oven would go up in flames again. This time the fire department was summoned, and my apartment building of four hundred people had to be evacuated. When the sirens started screaming, I was too embarrassed to go outside. I knew there wasn't any real danger; only butter that burned in the pan and caused enough smoke to set off the alarm system in the building.

I cried again, but my mom wasn't there to comfort me.

The Yankee and I had just moved from Boston to Seattle. He let the firemen into our apartment, explained what had happened, and allowed me to hide in the bedroom until the commotion had cleared.

From the window in my bedroom I could see all the people from my apartment building out on the sidewalk. Some of them decided to bail on the evacuation and walk to a bar across the street. We were living in a neighborhood that had a bar or restaurant hidden around every corner.

I wondered how I had ended up hiding in my bedroom instead of drinking and eating in public. After all, it was a Saturday night. But since we'd moved, I'd taken to cooking at home, so much so that we hadn't tried a single one of the restaurants on the city blocked where we lived.

Once the firemen left, my boyfriend came into the bedroom and looked at me until I spoke. I had been cooking dinner for us when the fire started. Not because he asked for a home-cooked meal, or because I was in the mood to stand in front of the stove for an hour, but because I assumed it was something that I *should* do for him. We had a domestic partnership now—all the forms that allowed us to share health insurance would attest to that. I thought I had a responsibility to be, well, *domestic*.

"Should we go out for sushi?" I suggested.

He smiled, and was kind. "That's exactly what I'm in the mood for," he said.

I still had the spatula in my hand. I had gripped the handle so tight that my wrist was cramped up by the time I finally had the sense of mind to drop it. Again, my eyes were lined with pink.

I couldn't muster the courage to ask if sushi was what he'd wanted all along. Or whether I'd set off the alarms and interrupted everyone's evening all because I'd created a story in my head about what I should be doing in the kitchen when what I

— 87 —

CALL ME A FOODIE

really should have been doing was peddling my bike around the neighborhood and looking for a new restaurant to try where people would cook dinner for me. Instead of spending the evening feeling trapped in my own kitchen.

Lesson: Take nothing for granted when it comes to food and love. Especially if you think something is obvious. Question that even more.

Best Paired With: Chocolate chip cookies. But not made from scratch. The kind that come prepackaged so that all you have to do is slice and bake. Or if you're like me, slice and burn.

Every summer when I left my parents to spend two weeks at Camp Grandma, I'd run gratefully into my grandmother's embrace and a warm slice of her pecan pie, happy to spend some time apart from my mother, my father, and all the boring vegetables they made me eat.

At home, there were no seconds on dessert. At Camp Grandma, dinner could be nothing but dessert. Every time I arrived, there was a countertop designated as my own and covered with foods she had prepared for me. And if I went downstairs to the deep freezer, I would find backups of these foods that had been frozen in case of a natural disaster (my grandma's worst fear), or in case my parents forgot to pick me up and take me home (my favorite fantasy).

The summer I first became curious about these dishes—how they were constructed, who had created the recipes, and whether they were available to grandchildren all over America, or just the very lucky ones in Texas—was the same year I started to ask questions about how she met my grandpa.

Before that summer, I'd never put much thought into how all those foods made their way from being ingredients in the grocery store to dishes on the countertop. They simply were a part of Grandma's house. In the same way, it seemed revolutionary that my grandpa might ever have existed without his beige recliner or crossword puzzles.

Was the cornbread in her stuffing homemade or bought from a store?

Had he been a strapping young man who swept my grandma off her feet?

I sat on the stool next to my countertop with one hand on the bowl of peanut brittle and a mouth full of questions.

Instead of answering my questions about cooking, she began to give me small tasks around the kitchen that would help me figure out the building blocks of cooking on my own.

As to my questions about she and my grandpa, she just told me that it all seemed so long ago and wouldn't we rather talk about what was happening now? So I would fill her in about all the boys at school who I'd started to notice lately, and why I was convinced that I was definitely the best candidate for first female president of the United States. Recently I'd discovered pictures of myself as a young toddler, when I'd been fond of wearing a T-shirt my parents' friends bought for me that said MADE IN MEXICO across the front. Not realizing I actually was "made in Mexico" and that it was a clever joke from my parents' friends, I thought it was simply a good omen for my future in foreign relations.

She kept my belly full of food and me full of questions to answer, so many that I got back on the track we usually stayed in—having fun in the here and now. I forgot about the questions I really had wanted answers to. What went into her dishes when I wasn't around? What were the makings of all the dishes that had made up my childhood summers?

The school year following the summer we had our soap opera-thon and I ate so much peanut brittle that surely my teeth should have rotted into a pre-cavity cave of petrified sugar, I went from being a rather cute and cuddly preadolescent who spent time with her family to teenager. As a teenager my time was to be divided equally between fixing my hair in the bathroom at home by myself, fixing my hair at the bathroom at school with my friends, passing notes about boys during class, and gossiping about boys after-school. Anything that fell outside those parameters was no longer a part of my world, especially spending time with my family.

From then on I would go to Grandma's house over the holidays with my parents and brother. But it was no longer possible for me to leave my social life for such a huge part of the summer. She and I talking alone in the kitchen was a thing of the past, and so my questions were left dangling indefinitely.

I only finally went back to Camp Grandma when I was twenty-eight years old. It wasn't the full two weeks, because working for The Man doesn't equal a lot of playtime. But I felt a sudden need to see Grandma one-on-one, and so I took a long weekend off, got on a plane, and made my first solo venture in a decade and a half to her East Texas enclave.

When I arrived, it was like old times, with some of my favorite foods on the counter. My grandmother hadn't been able to abridge all the recipes I'd requested to be vegetarian, but the ones she could salvage were presented to me. Of course, I couldn't eat dessert for dinner anymore. Not that I didn't love dessert—my metabolism was to blame. If that son of a bitch slowed down anymore it would practically be at a halt.

I offered to help her with dinner and she gave me some small tasks that would keep me busy just like she did when I was a kid. It had been a while since I'd cooked and I could sense that she detected my discomfort. You could have been wearing a blindfold and a pair of earplugs and detected my discomfort—a tin man has more grace. I fumbled with the knife before I chopped an onion and I carried a hot plate like it was a baby with a dirty diaper, so far in front of me I might as well have been passing it from East Texas across the Louisiana border.

"Do you cook very much these days?" she asked.

"No," I answered quietly.

It hadn't been more than a few years since I had actually cooked quite a lot. When I lived with the Yankee I'd researched ingredients and tried to memorize which spices worked well together. I searched for recipes online and would open cookbooks for fun. Back then I called her for advice frequently. But I'd stopped cooking, and calling, shortly after the breakup. The last recipe she ever gave me was the chili recipe I'd called for in the immediate aftermath. Oddly enough, I never even wrote it down, but I know it by heart to this day.

"You know, they say it can be cheaper for people who live alone to buy prepared food than to cook," I said.

I didn't mention the bowls of microwave soup, or the tubes of cookie dough I ate with a spoon instead of attempting to bake because I'd been burned too many times on something everyone else did so effortlessly.

"I suppose people do say that," she said. And then she let the conversation idle. She didn't disagree with me, but she didn't agree with that opinion either.

My cheeks grew warm and I kept my head down. If she was disappointed in me, I didn't want to look and risk seeing that in her face.

But then she spoke, "I've been cooking for two people for so long, I almost wish I'd never admitted I could do it in the first place."

Then she stopped her movements around the kitchen and just looked at me.

"What do you think is my biggest hope for you?" she asked.

"That I learn to cook?" I asked.

She shook her head no.

"That I fall in love again?"

Again, no.

"That I become the first female president of the United States?"

The look she gave me said that I was the only person who had ever really considered that a possibility.

"Joking," I said. "Not a good joke, just a joke."

This is what I always do when a joke has fallen flat. I call out that yes, that was a joke, a very stupid joke. Like when you meet a man who is bald and in the first two minutes of conversation he points out that he has no hair about sixteen times. I relate to those men. For whatever reason, announcing a shortcoming makes it feel less likely that someone will walk away and comment on how damn bald you've gotten in the last few years, or wonder when it was that you started making such awful jokes.

My grandma took a deep breath and at that moment she seemed tired. "In this life," she said, "I only want you to do things that you want to do."

She would not let me look away. When I tried, she waited until I faced her again.

"My friends and I didn't look around like you do. We didn't see all the options that were out there. We met men who wanted to take care of us and in return we took care of them back. All you *have to do* is take care of yourself."

"If you don't want to cook, then don't cook," she said. And then, "If you don't want to be with a certain man, don't ever pretend like you do."

Lesson: When you can't find the words, look for cheese.

Best Paired With: Lots of napkins.

Ignore what you hear on daytime TV or late-night infomercials peddling self-help literature. Emotional eating can be your friend.

Of course, if you eat a few extra bagels in the morning because you feel emotional about waking up late, and then you grab a slice of chocolate cake in the afternoon because you feel emotional about stubbing your toe, well, you can see how that kind of emotional eating could get to be a problem.

But if, let's say, once a year, you have the sort of emotional crisis that only lasts about twenty-four hours, but for that entire period of time you feel it's quite possible that the world might end. I've found that in those instances a large cheese pizza really can be a girl's best friend.

And emotional eating is not the sole domain of the individual curled up in the corner of her sofa alone. It doesn't just make one person's problems better—it can help a group, too. Let's say you've got people who just can't reach common ground or find the right way to communicate with each other. Maybe everybody just needs a nudge in the right direction from their taste buds. I can't tell you how many times I've been working a project with people I'd rather see dead than talk to for another day of meetings when all of a sudden someone drops a bag of bagels and cream cheese (heavy on the cream cheese part) in the conference room. The whole team relaxes and it becomes clear that the problem is that the clients are total assholes, and not that any of us are.

After all, we're humans. In our monkey days we used to communicate with each other by scratching our armpits and grunting. To occasionally tell someone you miss them by sending cookies, or perhaps that you are sorry for their loss by sending a casserole, isn't such a far stretch.

This is a lesson I first learned during high school in the cornfields of Oklahoma, right after I figured out that cows can't actually be tipped but beer bottles can be opened using a knife.

In all fairness, the state of Oklahoma is a fine place to go to high school, as long as you have friends. Whether you are friends with the football players, or the ranchers, or the brainy kids who would die if they ended up at a state school—and don't even say the words "technical college" in their presence lest they self-combust—it didn't matter. You were okay as long as you had a group, any group to hang with when those lonely prairie winds came whippin' through the high school parking lot.

I moved to Oklahoma late. Like eighth-grade late. Which is about eight grades too late if you want to fit into groups that have been established since kindergarten. Making friends wasn't easy. My early months there involved lots of lying on my bed and whimpering to my mother that no one liked me, but if I could get a brand new wardrobe then maybe that would yield a friend or two.

Of course, I didn't get the wardrobe, but eventually I did get some friends. And once I was on the inside of that group of friends, I found out that being on the inside of a group of high school girls wasn't a lot different from being on the outside. There was still the same alienation, occasional depression, and constant vigilance for an attack that could lead to your ostracization. Except inside the group meant you had people to go to the movies with on Friday nights, so I decided it was the better opinion.

And there's an interesting point: If you substitute a keg party for the movies, being in a sorority wasn't a whole lot different than being a hormonally instable and wildly insecure high school girl. Huh. Isn't life hilarious like that?

On Friday nights, my girlfriends and I would either go to the movies or tell our parents we were going to the movies, and then drive around our town, listening to music and trying to spot the good-looking guys from our school who were also driving around and listening to music.

When curfew arrived, we would drive to one person's house to spend the night. And because we'd already exhausted conversation about the good-looking guys, we often found ourselves at a loss for what to talk about.

With nothing to say and no one quite ready for bed, we'd usually end up eating.

We would cook frozen pizzas, and devour bowls of seven-layer dip. We'd go through bags of chips and the occasional pot of pasta. Our teenage metabolisms could handle this kind of eating, and our angsty, adolescent souls needed it.

We'd share food instead of offering up that each of us occasionally felt depressed. That each of us feared what would happen if one of those good-looking guys never looked back at us. That we wondered what would happen if we never made it out of that small Oklahoma town.

None of us had words for those fears. But the food did more than fuel our bodies, it bonded us together. Who needs a best friend's necklace when you have your best friend's cheese. Tortilla chips and bowls of melted Velveeta were just as invincible as two halves of a heart hanging on two sterling chains. We'd allow the food to fill the fear while we waited, together, for some answers about our future to finally appear.

There are days when it seems I have gotten wiser with age, but even with that wisdom I have not found words for all my fears.

People who have been blessed with perfect relationships don't know this, and I hate to be the one who pops the piñata and lets the real world fall all over their party, but here it goes. In some relationships there comes a point where a male and a female simply can't progress any farther.

No amount of talking, or fancy sushi dinners, or martinis will take this couple past the point. It's like an invisible wall that separates the people who really care about each other and will continue to feel that way forever, from the people who really care about each other but need to say goodbye. When you play other games for two, like checkers or chess, you might reach a similar impasse. Neither player can see any more moves, so it becomes a waiting game to see who will be first to stand up and walk away.

After the Yankee packed his duffle bag and moved out, I stayed in New York City for a couple years. During that time, I met a man who also went to the University of Texas. The mannerisms (and on occasion, manners) of a man raised in the South were buried under years of Manhattan living, but he liked to get drunk and tell people he was from Texas, and so we shall call him the Texan.

The Texan and I dated for months, even though the invisible wall could have been sensed from the start. I was looking for someone to replace the serious relationship I'd lost and the Texan wanted someone who would let him do as he wished, and then get together for dinner or beers when it worked for his schedule. I didn't want to acknowledge that the wall was there. And since it was invisible, on most days I found it quite easy and convenient to ignore.

On those days I thought that if I waited long enough, the wall would simply dissolve and he and I could live happily ever after forever and ever amen. Other times I wondered if I should push harder against the wall and try to push it down myself. And then there were days I simply wanted to bash the damn thing in with the toe of my cowboy boot.

But every night I hung out with the Texan we'd eventually arrive at that same point when conversation stopped and silence arrived. If we were every going to be a serious couple that silence would need to be filled with how we felt or what we wanted in life, or from each other. But there was always just silence.

We were never going to make it.

At the very end of our relationship, he and I ventured from New York City to Texas for a vacation. We visited Austin and then drove up to Dallas. During those three hours the silence settled over us again. We were having a fun trip, a very fun trip, but it was becoming impossible for me to ignore the fact that "fun" was the only thing holding us together.

I looked out the window for an hour and a half, watching the terrain that felt like home. I'd have to leave it in a few days for tall buildings, cement.

I'd grown so comfortable with the person next to me, too. But eventually I'd also have to walk away from him.

"I was thinking we should stop for kolaches," I said. Which wasn't actually what I was thinking at all.

He didn't take his eyes away from the road, or miss a beat. Texans take lots of things seriously: their gun laws, their monster trucks, their kolaches. "Breakfast, lunch, or dessert kolaches?" he asked.

"Any kind that has cheese," I answered. I closed my eyes and pretended we weren't already over.

"Perfect," he said, and put his hand on my leg. It wasn't pretending to him because this was all he had ever wanted.

We went back to our silence and I allowed myself to be comforted by the idea that we'd stick together for at least another day.

Lesson: A good foundation takes time to build. Speed through the first steps and you'll find yourself with an entrée that shakes like a soufflé and could collapse at any moment.

Best Paired With: Lasagna with noodles that weren't cooked enough in the beginning. And a couple bottles of merlot to wash down the mistake.

When I left college for Boston, the idea was that one friend from college and an office full of people would be enough foundation for a decent social life. As it played out, my one friend had a boyfriend who she really, really liked to stay home and watch movies with. And my office had about twelve people in it, most of whom were married with kids.

CALL ME A FOODIE

My first six months in town yielded very few friends, and even fewer dates.

Fast forward to a bar in downtown Boston a few weeks after Valentine's Day. I've met the man I actually like who will eventually become my boyfriend. The Yankee. We've gone on a few dates and not only is he cute, but I can also understand him when he speaks.

Most of the time, when one of these Northeasterners opened his mouth I felt like flagging down a translator to explain the Massachusetts dialect. Add to that my Texas drawl, which still comes out when I drink, and a flirtatious conversation could sound more like a UN meeting than two normal people trying to share witticisms over a Guinness.

But talking with this man was different. He thought my Texas accent was charming. When I told him that I decided to move to Boston before I could firmly pinpoint the city on a blank map of the United States, he laughed and said it was a brave thing for me to do instead of simply labeling it reckless or naive—words I had taken to using against myself when I was lying in the darkness of my apartment, attempting to fall asleep in a strange and cold city.

Before I could find a diaper for my verbal diarrhea, I was telling him everything I loved about the South, and the diatribe went a little something like, "Friendly people, the food, winters that aren't cold at all, the food. And did I mention the food, the food, the food."

For someone whose cooking during her entire four years of college was pouring cereal into a box, this flirtation strategy was rather bold—some might even say irresponsibly brazen. The smarter plan would have been to mention things I was actually skilled at. I could have said that people in the South play a lot of tennis, do great discount shopping, or are excellent at Mardi Gras.

"You wouldn't be interested in cooking some of this Southern food for me, would you?" he asked.

An understandable question, rewarded with a blank stare. Somehow our pints of beer had kept me from realizing that his question would be the natural next step for the conversation.

And then my pints of beer kept me from realizing my answer should have been, "No, because I can't actually cook." Or even, "Well, it would take a while for me to devise the perfect menu because I recently became a vegetarian." If I was scared of the truth, I could have at least given myself some extra time.

Instead, I took a drink of frothy confidence and said, *of course* I would be interested in cooking some Southern food for him. This was the first cute, intelligent, and intelligible man I'd met since I stepped across the Mason-Dixon.

"It'll be so much fun," I said, ignoring the caution, caution, caution blinking in my head. Usually the caution lights only appeared in times of major need, like when I was about to walk down a dark alley alone, or make a mildly-inappropriate joke at the office. That should have been my first indication that I was getting myself into a dangerous situation.

"Next Friday? My apartment?" I asked.

He agreed.

Then I took down the remaining three-quarters of my beer in two gulps and announced I would be catching a cab home right then, at that moment, pronto. I had six days to either learn how to cook or decide that I could stand the idea of parting ways with the only man who had quickened my pulse in months. Hell, who was I kidding, it was enough that he was a man with a pulse: I'd have him a feast by Friday if my grandmother had to fly up and cook it herself.

In the end it would have been more efficient—and probably a lot less stress on my dear grandmother—if I had purchased her a ticket.

CALL ME A FOODIE

I called her from the bookstore where I went to look for Southern vegetarian recipes (Which vegetable would be easiest to fry?), from the grocery store where I bought the ingredients (Does it ruin dessert if I can't find Blue Bell ice cream?), and then from my kitchen during the two nights I practiced the dishes I would cook for the actual dinner (Could I substitute vegetable broth every time the recipe calls for chicken broth?).

Eventually, my mother had to call and remind me that my grandmother was used to living with long periods of silence.

I summoned all my peace and calm as I reminded my mother that my life in Boston was introducing me to long periods of silence. *And that this dinner was the chance for me to break that pattern.*

In the end, there were collard greens and jalapeño cornbread and meatless stew with extra Texas spices. I made a small batch of okra that added that succulent scent of the South—fry grease. Which promptly settled into the crevices of my small apartment.

There was a lot we didn't know about each other, but this meal fast-forwarded past a lot of it. Different religions, different upbringings, different goals for our careers—let's finish the cornbread and focus on what a novelty each of us is for the other.

I started cooking for us more and more often, whenever there would be stress or a problem that would arise, without considering whether I should face the difficulties instead of looking to the kitchen to avoid our problems.

To deal with them might have meant a return to the loneliness of my first days in Boston, when it felt so bad to lie in bed alone. The fundamental ingredients weren't there between he and I, but I kept trying to add new ones on top, to mask what was missing.

Some cayenne in the bedroom.

A little salt in conversation.

Pepper to keep us on our toes.

Time and again I would take the concoction out of the oven, and taste to see if I'd finally hit on a combination of add-ons that could make it seem like nothing had ever been missing at all.

Lesson: If you don't have heart for something, it will always be revealed in the finished product.

Best Paired With: A glass of wine from a bottle opened a few (or maybe it was four) nights ago, followed by sex you only agree to because it seems vaguely more interesting than reading a book.

The Southern meal I pieced together in my Boston kitchen launched my life with the man I would live with for two years. And it took four years of dating before that for it to occur to me that neither of us was living, nor having very much fun.

It was after we'd moved into our Brooklyn apartment that I looked around our newest urban nest and realized I had baked myself into a corner.

All around me were the signs of a happy, yuppie couple. We had all the right magazines laid on all the right pieces of furniture. Every detail chosen because people who never spent time inside our apartment would have approved.

There were pictures on the wall—vacations to Rio and California, as well as trips to see family. We had a living room and a study and one bed where we slept facing a window that got beautiful daytime light. Our kitchen was well stocked, and I retreated there almost every day to cook something that, by the time I was done cooking, I'd lose interest in.

It didn't take long before our faux-life started to show very real cracks. But life in New York City gave us plenty of other places to look.

I was working from home, so during the day when I wanted to procrastinate I'd put together a menu for the night.

On one day in particular I wanted comfort food, so I pulled an old casserole recipe that belonged to my grandmother.

What I really wanted was to go out for dinner that night, but when I called the Yankee's phone he didn't answer. And so I constructed the casserole and waited for him to come home.

I waited.

I waited.

I waited some more.

The hand on the clock kept ticking, but my phone stayed silent.

I ate my dinner on the couch with a magazine open in front of me.

I chewed slowly.

I wondered if this was the scene Michael Cunningham channeled when he wrote *The Hours*. Housewife waiting. Dinner growing cold. Paralysis setting in.

This lifestyle was precisely what I thought I was avoiding by staying away from the suburban cul-de-sacs and white picket fences of my youth. Wasn't that the point of all the modern furniture? Sharp edges to poke the eyes out of the mundane.

Eventually he came home.

But even when he got home, he didn't act like he wanted to be in the apartment with me. I couldn't argue with that. I'd been having my own doubts about being in the apartment with me.

He'd already eaten so instead of saving the casserole I scooped the last of it into the sink as I listened to him make his way to bed.

Then I flipped on the disposal and let it destroy the food for much longer than necessary while I watched the New York City night from the tall rectangle window in the kitchen.

Sadly, there isn't a recipe in the world that can teach you how to make passion.

Lesson: The perfect dish is in a constant state of evolution.

Best Paired With: My grandmother's pecan pie. In forty years, she has never made the exact same pie twice.

These days I have settled into a pretty comfortable pattern of not actually cooking at all. I eat at home a fair amount, but I manage not to turn on the oven. It's safer that way—those blasted things are prone to fire.

My extended family was together in February at my aunt's house in Louisiana. And like we usually do when we are in Louisiana, everyone stayed up late. We entertained ourselves into the wee hours by drinking various kinds of alcohol, eating food, and chasing mosquitoes with fly swatters. Doesn't sound like your cup of tea? Then you best not marry a Cajun.

Once I'd gotten just tipsy enough to forget that I hated doing anything in the kitchen, I started to unload the dishwasher.

The conversation kept up. Laughing, drinking, talking, and I bustled around the kitchen putting dishes away. Before I knew it, my finger was bleeding.

"AAAAHHHHH!" I screamed. I had cut my finger on the knife I was putting in a drawer.

Immediately, all the conversation stopped. Everyone slowly turned to me.

"Are you okay?" my mom asked.

"Um," I said, holding my finger in the air, "I'm bleeding." I thought this was a fairly obvious explanation that I was less than okay.

"It does look pretty bad," my uncle agreed.

But still no one moved.

"Is someone going to come in here and take a look at it?" I asked.

There was silence all around. They all looked at each other and then my brother finally spoke.

"I think we were all just surprised to see you doing something productive in the kitchen."

I like to think it was more than just my drunkenness that kept me from holding a grudge against their delayed response to my injury. When my brother said that, it occurred to me that this was just the answer I wanted to hear. After my live-in relationship, when I'd turned cooking into a tie that would bind us together, I'd vowed to stay far away from the kitchen, and I'd achieved that goal to such an extent that the days when I aspired to be Betty Crocker had already fallen into the shadows of their memories.

Some women spend their whole lives in the kitchen and love every moment. Bravo. Clearly, not everyone can be eating dinner out—there are only so many tables in a restaurant. They can have orgasms over their first properly cooked pesto and I'll save mine for when the clearance racks at Target get stocked up.

I'm not sure exactly when I started to believe that a woman cooking for her man was a necessary ingredient for the relationship to succeed. Maybe it was after I spent my high school years believing that being skinny would mean that more people (read: guys) would like me. Or in college, when I thought that eating and drinking as much as I could would fill up the fear that I would never meet a man who loved me, though obviously a head start would have been to give a little of my own love to myself.

The food and the love, the love and the food. I suppose my mother is right and the two are wrapped up tight as a pretzel in my mental madness.

Who knows, maybe I will cook again one day. And maybe I'll enjoy it. I never want to give up the idea of trying something new, or falling in love with something that I previously declared off-limits.

If I meet a man I care about enough to settle down with, I won't believe I need to pave our path to happiness with recipes. It doesn't make me less Southern; it means I believe in compromise. (About cooking, not about movies. I always have impeccable taste in movies.)

But next time I do find myself doing something really weird with food—like turning into one of those people who only eats things that come raw from the ground, or investigating the world of macrobiotic eating—I'll probably take a step back and look at what's going on in my love life. Have I recently been dating a Rastafarian? Did I just go on a date with a guy who hasn't bathed in while and has too many biotics?

It's like my grandmother says, "If you aren't going to bother to learn from your past, there's no real point in struggling through any tough times that appear in the present." And now I will sleep easier knowing my brother did not ingest all those tira-mud-su pies in vain. I'll sleep longer knowing that if I accidentally sleep in past breakfast, maybe that simply means I'm destined to meet the love of my life while I grab an early lunch.

Chapter 5

Call Me a Wavemaker

A girl doesn't turn twenty-nine without at least a tinge of anticipation. It's the last year of your twenties. It's one last birthday to go wild before that big ole party pooper—*three*—comes and plants itself at the front end of your age. All you've heard are horror stories of gray hairs and ovulation medication and I'll be damned if a girl doesn't need to just let loose, have some fun, and forget that crows have feet. Obviously, *clearly*, it's a day best celebrated with your parents.

When I floated my idea of spending my twenty-ninth with my parents, I got reactions that varied from general acceptance to blatant mockery. When I divulged that we were in fact going to

Las Vegas, however, absolute incredulity set in from even the most supportive friends. No one could understand why I would want to spend my birthday with my parents in a town that prides itself on indiscretion. The gambling! The alcohol!

"Um," I'd ask these naysayers, "Have you met my parents?"

I have the blessing and the curse of having been born to people who could be six feet under the ground and still be more fun than I am. There was a family vacation once when my mother had Montezuma's revenge and even though her intestines were doing things that she forbids me from repeating to the outside world, my brother and my father still preferred to hang out in the room with her than with anyone else in the resort. It wasn't that they felt sorry for her, oh hells no. They simply felt my mother was the life of the party, even if her drink was pink with Pepto instead of the cranberry she usually pours with her vodka.

So my parents are fun. And they're great to vacation with. And they also seem to think my birthday is a day for their own celebration, too. Of course I totally disagree with that part, but do understand I owe them some credit for the whole sperm meets egg thing, so I don't raise too big of a ruckus around these types of disputes. When I started to think about who I wanted to hang out with for my twenty-ninth birthday, it just kind of made sense that I would travel with them. To be honest, I didn't think about the whole Las-Vegas-may-not-be-the-number-one-family-destination-due-to-inordinate-amounts-of-breasts-shown-on-a-regular-basis thing. And maybe I should have considered it, because the last movie my father and I successfully sat through together was *¡Three Amigos!* And I'm pretty sure the fairly modest ass-slapping made us both very uncomfortable.

But I asked them to go with me and they agreed. My parents have been to Las Vegas so many times (kindly refer to the above information about them being Way More Fun than me) that they had gotten a chance to try out all the hotels they were interested in. They knew that my only experience in Vegas was as a part of a bachelorette party, in which I'd stayed at a hotel that used HBO as a main selling point and where I was scared to drink out of the cups without a straw—all of which were of the bachelorette, aka penis, variety. At twenty-nine, the bad news has already arrived and you know damn well you're never going to be a president of the United States. There's no choice but to accept that your birthday is as close as you'll ever get to having your own holiday. To say the least, I was in the mood for a hotel upgrade.

After talking to people who had traveled to Las Vegas as adults—and not just in a crazed group of girls high on soon-to-be holy matrimony—I chose the Mandalay Bay. Not because the hotel is pretty. Or because the casino is something special. I picked Mandalay Bay as my birthday destination for one simple reason: I discovered they had a wavepool.

I had it stuck in my mind that I loved wavepools. Kind of like how you tell yourself geometry wasn't so bad, or maybe that the bitchy cheerleader at your high school was actually kind of nice until you pull out your old yearbook and remember that she wrote "good luck with the college guys" when *she* was the manipulator who had taken your high school boyfriend. To think that with time you'd almost given her a hall pass on her awfulness.

I had fond memories of spending youthful summer days at water parks. My friends and I would go to beat the Texas heat with lazy rivers, statues that shot water into the air like sprinklers, and wavepools that ran every fifteen minutes. The calm was always followed by waves that would pull you up and shoot you down.

In fact, the memories were more than fond, they were downright happy. And so I was shocked when I woke up early on the day of my birthday, put on my bikini, walked out to the wavepool, and—before I had even touched the water—was hit with a tidal wave of fear.

CALL ME A WAVEMAKER

Most of Las Vegas was still in bed, so the pool was not crowded. But because there were only nine or ten heads bobbing in the huge expanse of water, when the waves reached up, those heads completely disappeared in the sea of chlorine. My stomach tightened. I took in sharp breaths while I waited for these strangers to resurface.

I turned to my mother, who was more than a little annoyed to be up so early. "Why does that look scarier than I remember?" I asked.

"I thought it was weird you were so attached to the idea of the wavepool," she said as she yawned. "You were always more of a lazy river kind of girl."

I looked back at the wavepool, and the reality came crashing through my fond nostalgia: me, standing where the water hit my thighs, while my friends ran full speed ahead. I'd grab onto the rail on the far side of the pool and let it guide me to where my friends played. They thrashed in the deepest water, fearless. The wave machine would click into a cycle and start to make waves. They cheered and I peed my pants.

"I think I need a drink," I said.

"It's ten in the morning," my mom replied.

"And?" I asked.

"And, Las Vegas time, that means we're already running late for our morning cocktails," she finished.

"That is precisely the reason I risk permanent social-ostracization by still vacationing with you and Dad," I told her.

"And here I was thinking you chose us because you didn't have any friends who could endure the July heat in Vegas."

I would have claimed she was wrong, so very wrong, but it was the anniversary of her pushing me out of her birth canal, so I let her have the victory.

We spent my birthday morning, afternoon, and late afternoon lying in chaise lounges in front of the wavepool. My mother read her novel. I stared at the water, listened to people scream with glee, and occupied myself with the number one pastime of travelers to Las Vegas—the confrontation of demons I'd thought were long gone.

The thing is, my mom was right. I *was* always a lazy river kind of girl. For most of my childhood, and adolescence, and then early twenties, my preference was to go with the flow. Not causing any problems. Biting my tongue. Instead of speaking up, I would stay quiet, never wanting to be considered a wavemaker.

The first time I learned this lesson I was ten years old. And it wasn't a lesson I had to learn twice. My father had threatened to wash my mouth out with soap many times, but up to that point it had always been a joke. I would say, "Mom makes better dinners than you do," or ask "When can I have a baby sister?" My dad would answer, with a smile, "Watch that, or I'll wash your mouth out with soap," and we would all laugh.

Ha, ha, ha.

A family joke that belonged to our family.

Ha, ha, ha.

Ha.

When the chalky taste hit the roof of my mouth and the square bar touched my teeth, I wasn't laughing anymore. The bar of soap didn't hurt, but the shock made tears swell my eyes fuller than the heart of a Baptist on a Sunday morning.

I did everything I could to keep from swallowing the soapy suds; I imagined it was rainwater dripping off the gutter of my house—if I swallowed, dirt and frog poop would be in my belly.

It probably lasted two minutes but it felt like twenty. The moment that bar of soap was out, I leaned over the sink and spit until my mouth couldn't make any more water. My dad disappeared and my mom took his place with a comforting hand on my back.

"I hate him," I mumbled.

"No," she said, "you don't hate him. You just hate that you got in trouble."

It was official. No one was on my side.

Getting in trouble was for boys who looked up girls' skirts on the playground, or the one kid in our class who had already discovered his true love—the packs of Marlboro Menthols he stole from his mother's supply.

Trouble didn't come with the territory of being a good little girl. I buttoned my shirts all the way to the top button and wore knee socks, turned in my math homework on time, and rarely had a mean word for anyone except my imaginary friend, Lily, who had the damnedest habit of annoying me after I'd spent a whole day being sugar-sweet to everyone else in my life.

But that day I'd crossed the line that separated the good little girls from the girls who would grow up to date men on motorcycles and not spend Christmas with their families. I'd opened my mouth when I should have left it shut tighter than a metal trap on the ass of a coon.

The incident started with another girl at school who accused me of going through her purse when she wasn't looking.

Like most eleven-year-old girls, my friends and I were obsessed with being older. And to us, "older" meant being a teenager. Teenage girls were our idols—their purses, their eyeliner, their legs that didn't have hair.

We carried our mothers' old purses to school, thinking we had something in common with high school girls. Unfortunately for us, the hand-me-down purses were oversized and made us look more like the senior citizens we saw pushing walkers down the aisles of the grocery store than the seniors we were really attempting to emulate.

The girl who accused me of going through her purse was a friend of mine. To be most accurate, she had been a friend of mine the day before—the day I'd given her my key ring to hold. A staple among my favorite belongings, my mom had given me twenty odd keys on a ring so I could fill my purse with real-ish accessories. My mother apparently collected old, useless keys because not one of the keys actually matched a lock in my house. I knew because I'd tried them all.

When this girl decided she was mad at me for a reason I don't remember now but am sure was of vital importance at the time—because what doesn't feel vital when accentuated by the hormones of a junior high girl—I asked for my key ring back. She refused. And then, in front of all the kids who had paused their own recess play to watch our drama, I reached over, unzipped her purse, and then stuck my hand inside so I could get the key ring out for myself.

By the time she reported the transgression to our teacher, my ex-friend made it seem as though I had gone through her purse when she was not looking, even though every pair of eyes at recess was watching our argument and saw how the interaction actually unfolded. It's been, oh, you know—a couple decades. But it's still crucial that everyone knows how *right* I was in this schoolyard scuffle.

And by the time the teacher retold the story to my mother on the phone, she made it seem as though my intention had been to steal. (Even though I hadn't even gotten away with *my own* key ring.)

When it comes to making waves, not doing your homework is a swell in a pond. It's when you start messing with the Ten Commandments that you discover what it feels like to walk headfirst into high tide.

After school that day, I lay in front of the television with my knees tucked to my chin. I was exhausted from attempting to explain the real story to my teacher, my mother—all these adults who were supposed to be smarter than us kids but who still couldn't understand why my ex-friend was wrong and I was right.

My dad arrived home from work and immediately sat on the sofa. For two seconds—the average amount of time a man can stay quiet when he has something to say—he pretended to watch the television with me. Then he asked what had happened at school that day.

I couldn't go through the story again. My emotional resources were drained. The rights and wrongs and words in my brain all got mixed to mush and the top flew off my temper. "I am not a stealer and I hate everyone who says I am. Including you!" I screamed.

He hadn't technically said I was a stealer. But given how everyone else had reacted, I knew it was only a matter of time.

He asked if I wanted to talk about it like a grown-up. And, of course, I did not. I wanted to yell at the entire world (which at that moment, consisted of my father, my mother, and Lily, who was hiding out behind the television). I wanted everyone to know that things had been *fine* until my *stupid* ex-friend made a *stupid* stealing accusation that only *stupid* people believed.

Perhaps because I rarely yelled, once I started it was difficult for me to stop.

"You're talking back to me," my dad said calmly.

And I didn't take the warning as seriously as I should have. "Youaren'tlisteningtome!" I screamed.

"You. Are. Talking. Back. To. Me," he said.

My scream elevated to a shriek. "Nooneeverlistenstome!"

If karma is a bitch, it will require either a mighty pair of earplugs or a mighty bottle of scotch for me to raise a kid.

Before I knew it, my father had scooped me up and was carrying me back to the bathroom where the soap, the linoleum, and the punishment for girls who make waves were waiting.

His great-aunt had used soap made of lye when she washed his mouth out "for giving her lip." I'd heard the story many times. How the lye had burned so bad he never brought another four-letter word into her house again. Even now, as a fifty-year-old man who weighs

— 114 —

a hundred pounds more than that dear, old lady, he swallows curse words like he did those lye bubbles so many years ago.

He spared me the lye soap, but that didn't save me the sting. For days after my mouth-washing, the soap lingered in my throat like a thin film of guilt. I started saying I was sorry, hoping that the right words would make the chemical taste go away. I apologized to my father for talking back. Then to my teacher. And finally to my ex-friend, who immediately became my friend again and returned my cherished key ring.

Like my father swore he would never curse in front of his great-aunt, I vowed it would be a long, long while before I'd think about making waves again. And with Lily as my witness, I stayed true to my word.

Before I continue, I must clearly state that these are merely my own thoughts, and not an attempt to rewind decades of feminine advancement. I am all for bra-burning and birth-control-pill-taking and women in equal positions of power—whether in a boardroom or the bedroom.

I'll be the first to support a woman who isn't afraid to bust her way into the boys' club, or explain to one of the good ole guys in the office that it's her way or the highway. Bring on single women in sperm banks, and Mr. Moms, and all other positive results of women's liberation movements. I've been a feminist since my early days of *Mary Poppins*-watching, when Mrs. Banks marched out of her house and away from her kids in the name of women's suffrage.

I know many women sacrificed so I would not suffer a slow death by white kitchen aprons and matching picket fences. And I thank each and every one of them.

But I did not arrive on this earth with brass balls. If I could do it all over, I'd definitely ask for a pair. Hell, I'd ask for a few pairs, because I've dated more than a couple men who could use some.

CALL ME A WAVEMAKER

The unfortunate fact of the matter is that I was not lucky enough to start out with the ability to stand my ground.

Sure, the fact that I was born and bred a Southern girl has a little something to do with my tendency toward the demure. But the South isn't the whole story. I've seen East Coast girls rough as sandpaper who turn into silly putty when it's time to stand up to their men. And Midwestern women—as solid and sure as the day is long—who can't find the nerve to tell a pushy friend to stop pushing so damn hard.

And sometimes it's obvious when I approach something from a Southern perspective. I see that I am being too shy, too prim, too proper, because I grew up in a part of the country where women raised "chitlins," men toiled at offices, and eyebrows raised when ladies of a certain age were not yet married.

But occasionally the Southern tendencies aren't so easy to spot, and I can't decipher the exact reason why I am biting my tongue instead of making waves. In these moments, there's no separating the Southern part of me from the female part of me. Dividing all of that from the part of me that's slightly neurotic and prone to eating massive amounts of chocolate when I get nervous? Well, I'd estimate that at damn near impossible.

So I apologize if anything I say is taken as a subtraction from the larger cause—the intention is surely not to position women as moving backwards, it's to tell the story of me moving forward.

For a while after the mouth-washing, it was easy enough to keep from making waves. Instead of talking back to others, I saved up every contrary thought from the school day and then fired them at Lily like an automatic weapon on a firing line. But then I received devastating news—I heard through the grapevine that having imaginary friends could keep you from making real ones.

I asked around and I found out this was true—Lily would kill my social life faster than admitting to the collection of miniature bones I'd dug in my front yard. One girl told me in plain terms

JUST DON'T CALL ME MA'AM

that talking to an imaginary friend was no different than talking to yourself. Then she gave me a crucial tip for schoolyard survival that I still use at cocktails parties today. "You should really try not to be so . . . weird," she whispered. (If ever you see me looking a little lost by the cheese plate, it's likely that's what I'm repeating to myself over and over. *Try not to be so weird, try not to be so weird.*)

I had to say goodbye to Lily. But with her gone, there was no one to bear the brunt of my repression. I couldn't sit in the backyard after school and scream all my frustrations, because no one was there to listen. And so I started down the path already blazed by other hushed souls—I began to Swallow My Words.

Many people don't know this, but Swallowing Your Words is much more than an overused cliché. It's actually a highly effective way to develop deep, passive aggressive feelings. Swallowing Your Words has been around for ages. It's hard to pinpoint precisely how long, but a safe estimate would be since the days of Not Speaking Until You Are Spoken To.

Short of becoming an A-list celebrity, or being a B-list celebrity who somehow manages to date an A-list celebrity, it's the most thorough method around for completely fucking up your psyche.

Behavioral transformation of this magnitude cannot happen overnight; truly becoming one who swallows words happens in phases.

Phase One is when you find yourself wanting to say something contrary, but before you speak, you look around, evaluate the people in the conversation, decide that it is in your best interest not to make waves with these people, and remain quiet.

This happens a few times. You realize that by staying silent you are getting along great with people. Acceptance gives you the warm fuzzies and you think, *I didn't really need to share that opinion anyway. If I don't have anything agreeable to say, I shouldn't be saying anything at all.*

Maybe one of your new friends invites you to coffee, or to play golf. In my case, schoolmates stopped looking at me like I had frozen snot on my face and started letting me sit at the lunch table with them. I'm not the first to say it, but I'll preach it: Popularity is a powerful tonic. That rule applies for all pre-adolescent girls and anyone with upward aspirations on the ladders of corporate America.

Phase Two is when you have something funny to add to a conversation, but you're so used to looking around and evaluating your audience before you speak that you wait too long to deliver your joke and when you do, the timing is off, the joke falls flat, and you start to wonder why you didn't just swallow your joke along with all the other aggressive words now living in your belly.

Essentially, Phase Two is when the positive words get kicked off the wagon to join the aggressive ones in the ditch, and your vocabulary gets redecorated from a red sofa with yellow accent pillows—kind of quirky, maybe to some people downright hilarious—to a beige leather chair that no one is especially interested in but everyone tolerates because you have to be a real asshole to make a serious argument against something so easily forgotten.

I entered Phase Two during high school. Not coincidentally, around the time I actually started dating men instead of just having long, drawn out Cinderella-type relationships with them in my mind. He loves me, he marries me, we have kids, we live happily ever after. My mind was not so complex in those teenage years—a well-oiled (I blame it on the hormones!) machine on a search for the path of least resistance.

One of my first boyfriends—the Football Quarterback, known to my father as the Hood Ornament—wasn't really *into* sarcasm. So instead of making jokes at the expense of our small town, or about our tendency to go on the same damn date every damn night, I cut cynicism out of our conversations. I would end up calling him on the phone to say things like, "You were so hot last night when you threw that one pass, that really long pass, to, like, the end of the field."

(Which, in hindsight, is actually pretty funny. But I wasn't intending to be at the time.)

The highlight of that relationship was when he told me he loved me. In those days that was a big damn deal. The gossip circles kept a closer watch on whether a guy touched on the L-word than if he touched his girlfriend's breast.

Obviously I was elated. Him loving me was the first step in my four-step plan to happily ever after. Except at the end of the school day he found me at my locker. I was all bright-eyed and bushy-tailed, a girl who was *loved*. This only lasted a few moments because sometime between homeroom and science, he'd experienced a change of heart.

"I might have spoken too quickly earlier," he said. ("Ish", okay, this is *the gist* of what he said. I was hormonal and distraught and sixteen and this is the way I remember it, damnit.)

He told me he'd spoken too quickly, that he was fairly certain he didn't love me but that he definitely still wanted to stay together.

I wish I could say that I was making this up. Or at the very least that this was some kind of elaborate joke played in high school and—ha, ha—I wasn't actually this lame, but I was. My father called him the Hood Ornament. He didn't get sarcasm. This conversation was a completely real and pathetic after-school special that, oh wait, was actually my life.

I did not speak my mind to him. I did not tell him this was rather lame, or request that he rethink that statement. I did not threaten to break up with him because I'd already passed notes (this was WAY before text messages) to all eight of my closest friends letting them know it was pretty much a done deal and he and I would probably be spending forever together because he loved me. Nope. I just took it. Stayed with him. And consoled myself that love was just a fickle, fickle flower.

In case you are rooting for the girl who believed in love—and even as the girl who believed in love, I really don't think you should—a couple weeks later I received a special floral delivery of yellow roses and a card that read, "This time I mean it. I love you."

To this day, when I see yellow roses a little part of my soul shudders. They were the proverbial blood diamonds of my high school years, the reward for simply accepting whatever was thrown my way.

I remember my silence with regret, but people who swallow their words aren't bad people. They're just people who feel the world doesn't always want to lend an ear.

And if you spend long enough believing that the world would rather you stay silent, it's inevitable that you'll eventually start sharing this service with others—whether they've asked for this help or, much more likely, not requested it at all. Welcome to Phase Three.

I'd pinch the arm of a friend before a snappy insult from a bitchy McDonald's employee evolved into an argument. "Ha-ha," I'd say to the employee as I forced my friend out the front door. "That sure is funny. Yes we have been here every day for the last week to enjoy an ice cream cone, and yes, perhaps we are here more than you are. Yes, even though you are an employee. Like I said, sure is funny."

Then I would push my friend onto the sidewalk and shut the door before she could let loose and tell the bitch that she wouldn't know a cow if it dropped manure on her overly-eyeshadowed face.

Conflict avoided for my friend, and therefore for me.

Phase Four is when things get physical. In this phase a person goes from just staying quiet and theoretically swallowing words, to actually, physically swallowing deeply instead of speaking.

When I entered Phase Four, a lot of people would stop in the middle of conversation and ask if I was okay.

"Who, me?" I would answer. "Totally fine, just have a little something stuck in my throat."

Not entirely a lie, usually it was a bit of a Fuck You tickling my larynx.

All these words rumbling around in my body with nowhere to go very quickly escalated to Phase Five—which is the final phase. Phase Five is when the bottom falls out of the entire enterprise. Different people explode in different ways. Some go catatonic. Some go goth. And others commit to four years of sadistic self-flagellation—also known as joining a Southern sorority.

After years of Swallowing My Words, the logical step was to celebrate that repression through sisterhood with a group of girls who had also been doing the same thing for their lifetimes.

Except college included an ingredient I had never played with before—hard alcohol. And liquor is like fire for people who swallow words. When I got drunk I would say things I never imagined would come out of my mouth.

Did I really hate being told what to do?

Did I dream of posting a manifesto of all the sorority secrets to the world—if only the world would care to read it?

Would I actually prefer to gouge my eyes with a plastic spork from the sorority house dining room than listen to another girl vomit after a meal?

Surely not. That was so opinionated, so contrary, so *not* me.

Had to be the alcohol talking, I would think to myself. After all, I wasn't someone who spoke. I just swallowed words.

And so I stayed in the sorority. For four years I wore the T-shirts, stood on the kegs, and wondered if I was the only person with a sneaking suspicion that she didn't fit in.

What does a blonde Southern girl who fears she doesn't fit in do? Well hell if she doesn't move to Boston. I didn't move to

Boston because I wondered if life was better above the Mason-Dixon. No, no, I would never say that to the people I loved who would live in the South forever. I blamed the necessity of moving on the fact that I wanted a job in the advertising industry.

I explained to people—my mother, my father, the flight attendant on my flight to Boston, anyone who would listen, really—that the best jobs were in bigger Northeastern cities. I don't know if I even had the courage to explain to myself there was more to the story—that I wanted new scenery, new people, the chance at a brand-new life.

Boston brought the Yankee into my life. He was a great guy in many ways, except one way that should have mattered very much to me: he had zero interest in spending time in the South. Would I turn my back on Texas to be with him? It was one thing to leave after college, and sure I had said I'd stay gone forever—but was I really sure that was okay? Without even realizing it, I said yes, by swallowing words instead of speaking up when he made jokes at the expense of—as my grandma would say herself—our bass-ackwards Southern ways.

"It's not that I don't want to see your family, it's just that I don't want to spend my vacation in the South. What do people do there anyway? Eat fried chicken? Sweat in the godforsaken heat?"

I was silent.

"Are you okay?" he would ask.

"Oh yes, I'm fine. Just fine," I'd say. With that damn Fuck You in my throat again.

It wasn't that he asked me to stay quiet, I made the choice to ignore how I felt for one year, then two, and before I knew it we were living together and moving all around the country, chasing his jobs and dreams. And that was how I woke up and found myself wedged in the middle of my twenties, still with no idea what it would sound like if I spoke my mind. In a massive misjudgment of geographical synchronicity with my personality, I

— *122* —

was waking up in New York those days—the worst place to be if you're in a rut of not speaking up.

And as it turns out, Swallowing Your Words doesn't keep you safe from conflict. It just keeps you in a bubble of silence. That bubble feels safe, like a place you could stay cozy in forever until a jagged edge comes along and pops your false security.

For me, that jagged edge was the only thing that could have shocked me out of silence—a shard from my broken-in-five-thousand-tiny-little-pieces heart.

When the Yankee moved out of the Brooklyn apartment we'd committed to share, I was left without the security of my bubble. And there was no other person to fill all the empty space that was suddenly in my reach. Just me, myself, and my own voice—if I could find it.

Thank God I hate television. Thank God he took all the good CDs with him. Because eventually I got so sick of the quiet I started to fill that silence with my own voice. Words I'd been swallowing for two decades bubbled up and I belched them out. And there were so many of them.

Angry words.

Aggressive words.

I called my best friend and told her I was talking to myself—and since that didn't totally freak her out, I let her in on another secret: Instead of rambling about his shortcomings, I seemed to be deducing that I wasn't a victim.

Sure he had broken up with me, but hadn't I been the asshole for pretending I could spend forever with that man?

Wasn't it all my fault that I'd walked away from my home, my family, and my friends?

I decided it was also a good time for me to come clean with her about our "romantic" trip to Brazil. We managed to go ten days without having sex at all. In one of the most sexual countries of the world!

CALL ME A WAVEMAKER

I realized I no longer recognized this person who was getting down to the truth instead of softening the edges with sweet, sugar icing.

My best friend took a moment of silence. "The trip was really ten days?" she asked. "No way it was a long weekend that seemed like ten days?"

Nope, it had been ten.

"Is there hard alcohol in your apartment?" my best friend asked.

"No," I said, "I came to these conclusions on my own. No vodka required."

"So you're sober?" she asked.

"Yes," I said.

"Well, you might need a glass of wine for the stack of emails I'm about to send to your inbox."

"Okay," I said, not quite sure about her intentions.

"They're emails I've been saving," she said. "You might think you're just starting to realize these things, but they've been popping up in between the lines of what you've been saying and writing for years. I saved them in hopes that this day would come."

And so I bundled up for the snow, went into the winter night, and bought myself a bottle of merlot. When I returned to my apartment, the emails were sitting in my inbox.

I drank that wine while I got reacquainted with the woman I'd been for the last few years. Emails sent to my best friend from my time in Boston, while I was on vacations, during my moves to Seattle and then New York. There—hidden between my constant reassurances that life was good and everything was rolling along at an easy pace—was a dictionary of the words I'd been swallowing for such a very long time. Everything I had avoided making waves about in the relationship.

All the time I spent with his family without him wanting to spend time with mine.

Believing that advertising was the end-all be-all. He did, I didn't. It's kind of a long story that's not very interesting at all, unless you're someone stuck with a 9-5 in the advertising industry.

Catholicism. This isn't a long story: He was Catholic and I was not (going to be).

During the month he left me in Seattle so he could start work in New York I'd felt lonely, very lonely, while I wrapped up the loose ends of our lives.

Every time the alarm went off that fucker hit snooze.

There was an entire alphabet of letters that made words I hadn't been speaking—it was time for me to stop Swallowing My Words and learn to speak up for myself. Even if it meant being single, even if it meant upsetting people, especially if it meant making waves.

I told my empty apartment he was **N**o one I needed to cry over any longer. After all, **O**lfactory glands don't lie and I always thought his dirty shoes gave off a vague—yet very detectable— scent of seaweed and, damn, how much did I hate his **P**laid shirts that made me feel like I was sharing the bed with a lumberjack.

The next morning I took this knowledge (and a fuzzy(ish) brain from my one(ish) glass of wine) into the outside world. I discovered that even though people were trapped in a city grid, they were not living in a prison of silence. Three girls on the sub-way were screaming about sex and men and how their men were going to shape up and start giving them good sex. I sat in the corner of the subway train, and I had a book in front of me but I couldn't take my eyes off them.

CALL ME A WAVEMAKER

Wasn't the elderly woman two benches down feeling offended by these vulgar mouths? Would the mom with two kids tell the group to keep quiet? Two of the girls got into an argument and neither backed down or showed fear until the third friend broke it up. "You bitches be damn crazy," she had said. And they all laughed.

You bitches be damn crazy.

You bitches be damn crazy.

I realized, holy shit, I want to be damn crazy.

There was nothing crazy about those girls. And if they were heading to crazy town then I wanted to hitch a ride. I'd kept quiet, acted sane, dotted my i's and crossed my t's for the last twelve years and I still ended up with flat tires on the bike I'd been trying to ride.

I'd been such a good little Southern girl—good grades, good sorority, better-than-good hygiene. "Yes, ma'am," "Yes, sir," "Yes I'd love a glass of iced tea—thank you, ma'am."

And then I grew up into an adult who lived away but still nodded her head to everyone back home that yes, yes, yes one day I want a husband and kids.

Yes, yes, yes one day I would return to the South—of course it was the only place that could ever really be home. Of course I wanted to live in spittin' distance to my family. Of course this whole career thing was fun, but would eventually take a backseat to baking a bun in my oven.

And then I would go back to my real life with the Yankee and nod my head yes, yes, yes, of course we were both happy with the life we had.

But none of those yeses were really what I wanted to say. Maybe I wasn't the good little Southern girl I'd always thought I was. Selfish words sat on my heart—words that might keep the doors of debutante heaven locked to me forever. There was a certain way to act and speak and answer questions so that you didn't rock the boat, but now I was finally ready to jump ship.

I had feared if I told people I had a feeling deep, deep down that I wasn't meant to fall in line, that they'd be lining up to wash my mouth out with soap. But here I was, without the husband or the kids or the schedule that everyone else adhered to, and no one was there to raise much of a stink at all.

If I'd found my voice sooner, I could have stood my ground for more conversations. But just because I was one of the last horses out of the gate didn't mean I couldn't still give the race one helluva run. I could put one hoof in front of the other and charge through all those awkward conversations—mane swooshing, head high, whinnying whenever the mood struck me.

Once I started dating again I would approach communication with the opposite sex in a brand new way—I'd actually communicate what I thought and how I felt. It wasn't going to be full-on Jerry Springer smackdown; there'd still be some gentle, Dr. Phil-esque two-way communication mixed in. It's just that I had finally made a decision. Instead of being the woman who followed along in conversation, I decided it was better to be a crazy bitch in the lead.

While I waited to feel ready to plunge back into the dating scene—after all, a girl needs time to lick her wounds, even if she does figure out she played a significant role in doing the damage—there was plenty of time to think about how I would handle dating conversations when they came around again.

The first conversation I had to make peace with was the big whammy of the dating world: The Breakup Conversation.

We're all supposed to fear The Breakup Conversation. It makes no difference if you're a regular gal like me or a virtual Venus like Angelina Jolie. When The Breakup Conversation comes up, inevitably someone goes down and the fear can be paralyzing.

CALL ME A WAVEMAKER

Let's say you fall in love with a book in the beginning pages but then you grow more sick of it with every page you turn. (If that's how you feel about this book, that's fine, but just don't say it out loud.)

You don't want to give up on the story, because really, you thought you loved it in the beginning and maybe you can rediscover what interested you at the start. By the end, you are reading into every word, wondering if you can return to the fabulous feeling of the first few chapters.

Single women of marrying and birthing age are supposed to do more than hold onto every word, we're supposed to turn the book upside down, see if studying the letters from a different angle gives a new perspective on how to reignite the passion. Under no circumstances are we supposed to put down the book, let alone walk away without a fight. It only takes a few late night infomercials to remind us that we're not getting any younger, and neither are our breasts.

I know the fear that arrives in the five minutes after The Breakup Conversation. I know walking away from the telephone, or your favorite booth at an Italian restaurant where the two of you always went on Saturday nights, or an email on the computer, as the realization hits you that your life has just changed in a big way.

When you're in the throes of the conversation that ends a relationship, it's difficult to remind yourself that this change is probably for the best. It's much easier to imagine yourself in twenty years with sixty-two cats feeding off a couple cans of tuna fish in your living room; the woman who qualifies for AARP membership yet still gives her mother's name as an emergency contact at the doctor's office.

In the past this fear would reach into my throat and press pause on The Breakup Conversation. I would be able to spy potential I'd never before seen in the man across from me. I'd be able to imagine what the two of us might be, if only we weren't, well, us. I'd convince myself to put off this horrible and awkward talk because what if he was more than The One to go bowling with or The One to enjoy martinis with and was actually The One to burp in front of for the rest of my life without shame, and I just hadn't found the right way to look at him.

Maybe his moodiness was a phase.

Maybe if we tried again in a new way, perhaps after some feng shui in his living room.

Maybe I could make myself into the woman he wanted, and he could just cut down on that habit he had of cupping his testicles while he watched TV.

Maybe he could pretend to be someone he's not and I could be someone I'm not. And together our fake selves could live fake happily ever after.

So the dreamer in me would create a fake ending that would never have anything to do with reality, and try to turn The Breakup Conversation into The Let's Give It One More Try Conversation. If he stood his ground I would use my sharpest verbal tools to dull his arguments and twist the truth. I would blindly ignore the little ping in my belly suggesting this end actually was a beginning.

I would think cats.

I would think mother as emergency contact.

But I didn't have to follow that script anymore. Now that I could start speaking my own mind, The Breakup Conversation didn't have to be something to fear.

Instead of picturing myself as a quinquagenarian cat lady, I saw myself choosing what I wanted to do on a Saturday night, and never again having to explain why it made good fashion sense for him to walk away from the sweaters his mother knit every Christmas.

Maybe my breasts were getting older, but that also meant my brain could be wiser. I would no longer paint rosy clouds over the gray horizon of the relationship—nine out of ten men who hold their testicles while watching TV will never give up the habit. The

CALL ME A WAVEMAKER

best thing was for me to get out before I committed in front of God as a witness to share a couch with that habit forever.

There would be no begging or crying or saying things that I didn't mean in an attempt to recreate the attraction we had felt in the prologue of the relationship. When I amicably agreed to The Breakup Conversation, I would be agreeing that sometimes things in life break, and not even the most fabulous feng shui can put them back together again.

The Breakup Conversation is a difficult conversation to master, but no occasion is as ripe for awkwardness as the ones you encounter at the beginning of a new dating relationship.

Before I could get involved again, I'd have to master the way to approach these dialogues. In the beginning of a relationship, someone is asking to know more about you but you aren't sure how much to share. You are vulnerable, exposed, and at any moment can be dismissed as not-good-enough for the person across the table from you.

There is The What Do You Want To Do With Your Life Conversation. (In more blunt circles, this is The Are You Successful Enough For Me Conversation.)

And then also The What's Your Dating Story Conversation. (In more blunt circles, this is The What Kind of Emotional Baggage Do You Carry Conversation and The Why Have Other People Previously Discarded You Conversation. A two for one of sorts.

Though the Southern girl in me has always enjoyed two Frito pies for the price of one, cramming two emotionally charged conversations into one has never contained the same level of cheesy, chili goodness that I found in that state fair snack.

Even if those conversations go well, you aren't rewarded with simple banter back and forth, oh no. As any dater worth her salt knows, after maneuvering the land mines of those first conversations, you will likely find yourself up close and personal with The Number Conversation.

Lots of people leave The Number Conversation in high school or college—as soon as everyone has enough experience to stop feeling insecure that they're lagging behind in some way. Admittedly, this isn't a bad resting place. As a person grows older, it makes sense that there would be no reason to divulge *their numbers* to another person. There's not a problem with it all staying private: The number of people you've kissed, the number of people who have touched one or more of your breasts, the number of vodka tonics you've had in the night, the people you've slept with after questionable numbers of vodka tonics. Not that I would know a thing about that.

Of course, the most important number to discuss for two consenting adults who are dating is the number of people they have previously consented to. But once everyone in the room is old enough to assume that that number isn't zero, then whether it skews to two or twenty shouldn't make or break the deal. (Assuming any sane person whose number skews to two hundred would take liberty to tell a lie in The Number Conversation anyway.)

Granted, if you're a girl who got hauled to her fair share of Vacation Bible Schools and Disney Matinees, it takes a bit of wind from the sails the first time you realize there's no Prince Charming saving himself for you. But once you get over the fact that your Cinderella moment will not be as the religious right intended, it frees you up to have some fun and you can skip over The Number Conversation.

Unfortunately for me and anyone I'd date from here on out, fun would not always be the primary part of the equation. Perhaps because of all the Vacation Bible Schools I got dragged to, and perhaps in spite of the happy endings I've endured at the hands of Walt and his fair princesses, I was ready to become a puritan "no pain no gain" dater. If there isn't a little awkwardness, then it wouldn't be worth staying for dessert.

Anytime I felt curiosity, I would flex my voicebox and begin The Number Conversation.

"Give me a ballpark," I'd say.

In the old days, I probably would have accepted any response that got thrown my way. Six, sixty-two. I'm a modern, occasionally hip by accident kind of gal, I could take it.

But I was no longer going to toe the line between good girl and independent girl, pulling whichever response would be most acceptable from my feathered fedora that I thought was hip but might have, accidentally, been a bit outdated. If his number was out of this world then I would give the first out-of-this-world response that popped in my brain.

"There are two possible reasons for how high your number is," I might remark after my disbelief (and coughing fit) subsided. "One is a nudist camp, and the other is being a part of someone's entourage. But that someone would have to be very, very famous. And possibly have twenty-four-hour access to a brothel."

And I would be fair about it all, I was not going to ask questions that I would not answer myself. When the number question got lobbed back my way I would answer and smile—confident in every decision I had made in past lives, past bars, past mildly drunken states.

It's a very non-adult conversation to have. But now that I could finally handle it like an honest adult there would be nothing to be ashamed of, nothing to feel bad for, or act embarrassed about. Maybe my newfound honesty would even give my date and I reason to make it through the entrées and get to dessert.

Previously in my dating world, dessert is the time when I either know I'd like to see this man again, or I know it's time to fold the night like a hand of poker gone wrong. Just like a hand of poker, sometimes dates go perfectly well until the last moment, and then they take a turn for the worse when the last card arrives. Identifying a date gone wrong gave me a lot of pain before I decided to throw timidity out the window along with the pair of jeans I'd been holding onto for three years *in case* one day they fit.

So much of me wanted to believe in second chances.

So much of me wanted to think that sometimes two people have more in common than they discover at first blush.

So much of me didn't want to be the one to hurt someone's feelings. I wasn't going to be the one to fess up to facts and say, "This date has been a real sonuvabitch. Let's take two tequila shots and go our separate ways."

But then things changed. I decided that tequila was occasionally as effective as tiramisu for dessert, and I learned that The Goodbye Conversation isn't as hard as it seems.

If you leave a Friday night date feeling like you need to recoup by spending a weekend on the couch listening to Dido and pondering the meaning of life, then you haven't commandeered The Goodbye Conversation correctly. It's a clean break with a firm handshake, and any emotional vampires who want to suck the life out of you with unnecessary follow-up questions and/or guilt trips need not apply.

Dido should only be listened to when remixed with Eminem, never as a cry for help. And for the love of God, never with your curtains drawn on a sunny day.

Once I finally figured out how to speak up, it was time to master the one conversation that didn't require voices at all. If you haven't dated since before a Bush ever set foot in the White House, then you may not be aware, but knowing how to text message is half the battle in today's dating world; a person must participate in text messaging or else risk all sexual organs slowly shriveling and shutting down from nonuse.

With all of the speaking up I planned to adopt in my dating life, I would have to take my newfound freedom into the digital age. But The Text Message Conversation is an entirely different beast than any other conversation for one main reason: In The Text Message Conversation sending no message is the loudest message of all.

With the advent of email and text, flirtation can happen instantly. These forms of communication appear to be more accessible. But this is a dangerous assumption—confident daters know that the dramatic pause is just as necessary in digital conversation as it is in face-to-face communication.

You cannot fall into the trap of believing that a man is making an effort simply with his text messages. He also needs to speak into his phone on occasion, instead of just typing. Sharing too much over email is just as dangerous. Long message chains can lead to a false sense of knowing a person—before you are even 100 percent sure what color their eyes are.

Now when a man texts me, even if he is the most delicious thing to come along since some genius put peanut butter chips *inside* a peanut butter cookie, I still wait at least a day to text him back. This isn't playing games; it's knowing that you are a person worth waiting for. And there is a lot more to you than can be communicated in the 140 maximum words allowed by Twitter.

As an intelligent, independent woman, I have a right to get past all the text messaging to an old-fashioned, in-person dinner date. After all, that is my opportunity to decide if I want to see how much baggage a man carries, what his number is, and whether I would like to invite him for a nightcap, or if it's an evening that's best left to a shot of tequila and The Goodbye Conversation.

No one has had more fun with me learning to speak my mind than my parents. Mildly amusing, on account of the fact that they watched me roam the earth as a fearful quasi-mute for years.

"I assumed you'd snap out of it," my mom offered.

"Just thought you were wired to be quieter than your mother," my dad said.

They admitted that the whole time I was living with my ex-boyfriend, my grandmother would wake them in the middle of the night with phone calls. The question of why I was letting "that damn Yankee get his way all the time" kept her up at night.

I accused my dad of starting it all with the bar of soap so many years ago.

"Hogwash," he said.

And I rolled my eyes in response. Although not a verbal response, per se, I happen to believe it falls under the category of speaking my mind.

Yes, both my parents watched as I learned to make waves in my personal life and applauded the change right until that meant standing up to them in Las Vegas on my twenty-ninth birthday.

That day we spent laying by, but not getting too close to, the wavepool, I floated the idea of not coming home for Thanksgiving that year. I was turning twenty-nine years old, after all, which to many people is considered to be the age of a fairly independent, functioning adult—the kind who can decide that fighting the airport traffic is too exhausting and she'd rather stay home with an individual serving of non-turkey Tofurkey than risk an altercation with the sort of traveler who believes it's acceptable to stuff three Gucci suitcases into the overhead compartment on top of the one fragile laptop you gingerly placed above your seat.

"If I had a husband and kids," I said, "you guys would never expect me to be home for every set of holidays."

They were all quiet for a second. Which happens, ironically enough, as frequently as Thanksgiving.

My mother spoke first. "Just marry someone who hates his family and there won't be a conflict. You can spend every holiday with us until we die."

"I'm serious," I said. "I want to see what it feels like to wake up on Thanksgiving without everyone around. And since today is

— 135 —

CALL ME A WAVEMAKER

the day we celebrate my birth, do you really have to bring up our imminent deaths?"

"Dad?" I asked. I thought I had a chance at his support. I forgot my mom had his gambling cash stowed away in her purse.

"There are two options I see here," my dad said. "You can either stop talking about skipping Thanksgiving because you are marching up to the bar to get me a drink, or because I've dunked your ass in the wavepool."

He tipped up the lid of the hat that keeps his nose from burning to a crisp and gave me a wink. "You're going to be with us this Thanksgiving whether you like it or not. It's a family thing. Which is, incidentally, why I'm having a pretty decent time even though I'm in Las Vegas during the hottest damn month of the year."

My mom smiled. I don't think it was because she won, but because she genuinely believed that being home for the holiday would be the best thing for me, whether I knew it then or not.

The gift they gave me that birthday was a lesson every person should have the chance to know—standing on my own two feet doesn't mean I always have to stand alone.

It was one thing to speak my mind, but making waves just for the sake of making them wouldn't make me more independent. It'd just make me into a stubborn ole mule before I'd even had the chance to say howdy to thirty.

Chapter 6

Call Me a Partner in Cohabitation Crime

My grandmother is on the other end of the phone line, but she's not saying a word.

This is a woman who taps her foot five minutes into the preacher's sermon, sure that she's thought of something he'll forget to add. She wakes up in the middle of the night and takes notes on what to tell people in the morning—unless you're a blood relative or you owe her money, then it's your responsibility to answer her phone call regardless of the hour.

"Never met a word I didn't like," she often points out. "Though I never had much use for 'Yankee.'" If you're from some place foreign, like up north, she'd serve you iced tea but as soon as you complain about the five pounds of ice or the five pounds of sugar she'd know she'd been right to have her suspicions since before you walked in the door.

Now she hasn't spoken for over three minutes. I know because I've been watching the clock since I stopped talking. She is giving me the Silent Treatment, and I have no choice but to hang on for as long as she does. No matter that I have to eat dinner at some point. And go to work the next morning. I'd stick a toe in a crocodile pond before I'd hurt her feelings by saying she's stubborn, but I was starting to wonder if this silent conversation would keep me from the party I'm invited to on Saturday night.

Just a few minutes earlier I was her granddaughter who could do no wrong. I walked on clouds instead of cement. I smelled like perfume even after a jog in one hundred-degree heat. Sure I'd moved to Boston after graduation, but that could be tolerated as long as she could tell herself it was a phase I was going through, something I needed to get out of my system. But now I was calling her from my kitchen in Boston after one year of a relationship with a Yankee—likely another thing she had believed would be a phase—and I'd managed to leave her speechless. I was doing the unthinkable, the unacceptable, the unforgivable. I made the one announcement never expected of a straight A-receiving, rule-following, raised to be God-fearing kind of girl. I wanted to move in with a man without a ring on my finger, not a preacher in sight, no way to legitimize any love that gets made.

I contemplate what she might say once she does finally decide to speak. We can't talk about sex. She would never want to make that part of my relationship equation real by speaking it out loud. Nor can we talk about what she probably does want to say—that this decision makes it more likely she won't be around when I finally

JUST DON'T CALL ME MA'AM

get around to getting married, not to mention having children of my own.

I've never received the Silent Treatment from her before, though I have witnessed its sobering effect on others. There was the Thanksgiving when Grandpa commented that the turkey was a little dry. She skipped over his compliments on the sweet potatoes and asparagus casserole and immediately assumed he was saying she might as well have served Big Macs for the holiday meal. Furthermore, he might as well have said that all the millions of meals she'd prepared during their marriage were dried-out pieces of cow dung.

She speaks to him now, which is good, because that Thanksgiving was over a decade ago and that would have made for too many silent nights of marriage. But my family and I often theorize about how long she ignored him. My parents think one week. But I'd sat in the kitchen with her while she spent all those hours preparing that turkey and I'd countered that it had to have lasted at least a month.

She gave my dad the Silent Treatment the summer he bought his Harley-Davidson. My father had dreamed of riding motorcycles since before he knew how to pedal a bicycle. When he turned fifty, he decided he'd waited long enough.

But Grandma prefers every vehicle to have as wide a berth as *The Mayflower*—then there's no question she can cross the intersection or the Atlantic without injury. Blue-haired ladies behind Buicks signal prudent safety. Leather-wearing men on crotch rockets signal, well, the exact opposite.

During the month she was recovering from the news of his new purchase, she only answered calls from our house because my mother, brother, and me still lived there. If she picked up the phone and my dad was on the other end of the line, she'd wait in silence until he passed the phone to one of us.

CALL ME A PARTNER IN COHABITATION CRIME

And then there was the Silent Treatment that I secretly sided with her on—the year my parents told her they were leaving America to move to Malaysia. I was in my early twenties and felt my own interest in travel and living abroad meant I couldn't speak up and say, "No, please, don't go." Because what if I wanted to up and move to Paris someday for a life of chocolate crossaints and cigarettes, would I want anyone to try to stop me?

And my interest in keeping up a guise as an independent adult kept me from holding onto my mother for dear life and saying, "If you must go, then woman, don't you dare leave me behind."

Grandma didn't understand why a person would ever need to leave East Texas and didn't seem to understand that Malaysia is a peaceful country in Southeast Asia and not a worn-torn Middle Eastern nation where my parents might feel unwelcomed. So she raised hell—which actually meant raising a wall of silence. My parents had no choice but to pack their boxes and plan the move anyway, hoping that by the time they flew across the ocean her temper tantrum would have ended and she'd be speaking to them again. I hoped so, too, because every time I tried to explain the difference between Malaysia and the parts of the Middle East that her FOX News stayed glued to all day, she'd stop listening to me and turn the volume on her TV up. They'd report danger and she heard Malaysia. I'd try to convince her of the peacefulness and kindness in Malaysia, and she heard danger.

In the end, Grandma usually does forgive. Whether she forgets is a debatable point, but bless her sweet-potato-bakin', turkey-bastin' heart, she forgives. Eventually she even went so far as to muse about whether she could make the trip to visit my parents in Malaysia, though we all secretly believe that conversation was fueled by one too many bourbon balls on a festive holiday afternoon.

In all the times I've watched the Silent Treatment from the sidelines, and celebrated that I wasn't on the receiving end; in all the times that I've slid up to Grandma like a sly little snake at the peak of her anger against someone else, to remind her how angelic I am, it never occurred to me that I would ever provoke the Silent Treatment. I don't use hard drugs and my job doesn't require me to exchange sex for money. She already made me swear when I was a wee lil' lass that I'd never get on the back of a motorcycle for as long as I lived. But here I am, receiving the Silent Treatment. And the Silent Treatment succeeds at what it is intended to do: I'm at a loss for what to do next.

Should I speak?

Should I apologize?

Should I ask if I can send her flowers, and maybe a year's supply of bourbon?

Eventually I hear her cough, which apparently is Silent Treatment Language for goodbye, because the line goes dead.

By now I've lost my appetite for dinner. And just for a second, I wonder if I've lost my appetite for moving in with this man I am certain I love, but am also certain I'm not ready to marry.

Of course, I didn't expect to call my grandmother, announce the news, and have her hallelujah through the phone. I knew pretty damn well she reserved hallelujahs for seriously celebratory situations—like when my little brother showed up for a visit with hair shorter than his shoulders, or when an upside-down cake comes out of the pan without going downside up.

But I had no idea she'd take this announcement as bringing shame on our household. We're a Southern family, not a Shakespearean one. I didn't set out with personal ads stating, "Seeking a man who is willing to share living quarters but not marriage, so my grandmother will be embarrassed to speak of me and refuse to speak to me." I was not expecting to be branded with a scarlet "**W**" on my chest—whether for **W**hore, or the only slightly less-inflammatory **W**ell-traveled vagina.

I had met different kinds of people than the ones I grew up around and saw all the different ways they chose to live. Suddenly there were options I had never considered. It was like multiplying five hundred possible life scenarios times five hundred variables and then trying to cipher through those for the ones that would make me happiest: Husband and no kids versus no husband and no kids but a domestic partner versus city life or country life or a life that volleyed between both.

It became impossible for me to believe that relationships were as simple as meeting a man, marrying that man, having children together, and then growing old and gray. Quite frankly, as a twentysomething who had her head spinning with options, I doubted my ability to commit to spending the next fifty years with a man without—at some point—taking a steak knife to his throat. I assumed everyone who knew I was exploring these options would see wisdom in the addition of a 'living together' step in the cycle.

There are people who excel at the approach of first comes love, then comes marriage, then comes a screamer in the carriage. But I was not the kind of person who woke up and greeted a new day with unbridled enthusiasm that lasted throughout the day. It was quite possible that my mood might change without just cause somewhere between five and eight times a day, and that those mood changes might mean the difference between whether I wanted to live in Manhattan or move to Muskogee. No, the simplicity of a lifestyle modeled after a nursery school rhyme wasn't flying.

In my opinion, the omnipresence of cable television in our day and age practically requires every citizen to be armed with the knowledge tendered on us by *Judge Judy,* and endless marathons of the *Real World,* or (gasp) by actually getting to know the people in our own neighborhoods. We should know that sometimes two people need their own recipe for staying together, one that might involve cohabitating before marriage so they don't end up separating later in ways that cause far more emotional damage (families torn apart by divorce and complex questions like "Who will keep the mobile home?") and financial damage (parents who never recover their 401(K)s after being gouged by the price of a wedding photographer for their daughter's nuptials).

I failed to realize that for all the marvelous things small-town East Texans (including my grandmother) are known for—close relationships with kinfolks, knowing how to cook snake so it doesn't taste so different from chicken—being open to social change in the traditional male and female dynamic may not be among the highest priorities.

I thought I was making an enlightened move. A responsible move. A move that would not land me or my boyfriend on *Judge Judy* anytime in the next three seasons. Yet my grandma thought I was making the mistake of a lifetime. In one fell swoop, I had gone from being something she could brag about to a reason for her to dodge friends at the shopping mall.

Instead of being a woman who could look with sorrow on friends whose grandchildren were pursuing deviant ways—majoring in art instead of something sensible like accounting or engineering, serving store-bought cakes to guests, wearing white long after Labor Day—I would be living in sin with the Yankee, and so she would be in a living hell.

And so I did what any self-respecting granddaughter on a fall from grace would have done: I panicked.

I immediately laid down on my kitchen floor and started to take deep breaths. I thought zen. I thought relaxation. I thought, *Shit, when was the last time I swept this fucking floor,* and hoped my inability to combat dust bunnies would not be a deal-breaker in my forthcoming domestic partnership.

My mind jumped to years and years before when I was at Camp Grandma, collapsed on her floor in a little ball of despair because my crush was in love with another. I wondered if I should give up the whole lying on the floor to stop the world from spiraling down thing. What did other people do?

Go to a bar?

Go to a shrink?

I'd rather stay on the floor, but damn it would have been nice to have Grandma bring me a piece of pecan pie while I was down there. Obviously, that remedy was currently out of the question.

At that point I concocted three possible courses of action to rectify my standing with Grandma, and convince her to speak to me again.

Option One: I could call her back and hope she answered. When she did, I could accept all blame for having made a bad life choice. Then I would simply call my boyfriend and tell him we weren't going to move in together because my Southern sensibilities were at odds with the decision. Which would result in him wondering aloud why my Southern sensibilities hadn't spoken up a little sooner, like, while we were making these plans for the previous three months. Which would likely result in us breaking up. Which would mean he'd get all the justification to hate the South that he'd ever wanted, and I'd end up eating canned soup on Saturday nights and using motorized devices to have orgasms. Which, at that point in my life, I imagined to be a miserable existence, but ironically, would have delivered better sex than I found in the relationship. Damn hindsight, always twenty-twenty.

Option Two: I could call her back and hope she answered. When she did I could explain that even though this decision was not proper in her eyes, it was the most proper move I could make for me. And then in the most mature, responsible way possible, I could ask for her to support me, and to respect the adult woman I had grown into.

Option Three: I could take no responsibility for the situation at all, continue to lie on my kitchen floor, and place the blame entirely on another person. Even better, instead of blaming a person who might be able to defend themselves or do something I really didn't want to deal with—like throw a bigger ball of blame back at me—I could be smart about it, and point the finger at something that would never be able to fight back.

After all, I hadn't rolled from the womb as a disgrace to my family. I didn't fall from the pedestal on my own accord—I was pushed by something. And lying there on my linoleum, the answer came to me: that something was the city of Boston.

Oh yes, I'd found the bull's-eye for my blame. It was because of *Boston* that my morals were now so offensive to my family. It was because of *Boston* that I'd deviated from the tried and true path. *I* couldn't be expected to resist the pull—*Boston*, in all its northeastern liberalness, was a centrifuge that had taken the respectable calmness of my life and turned it into a tacky tie-dyed T-shirt sold on clearance to summer tourists with tacky fanny packs milling all around *Boston*.

When I graduated from college in Texas I was like so many other college graduates—trapped by fear. I'd heard rumors that other college kids had spent four years learning and not just drinking. I didn't know if my sorority was something I should list on my resume or walk away from like a bad one-night stand.

I watched as people around me resolved their own fear with rational, secure decisions. Moving to Texas towns that weren't far from their families but still offered decent-paying, career-building jobs. Discussing marriage with long-term boyfriends. Renting apartments with luxury amenities like parking garages, high ceilings, and people they knew within shouting distance.

But my fear didn't make me want to settle, it made me want to speed to a new adventure.

But from the vantage point of your parents' house, the summer after graduating from college isn't the most hopeful place to be. It's like ramping a car up, up, up the hill of college only to get to the top and then not having any idea where to steer the vehicle.

CALL ME A PARTNER IN COHABITATION CRIME

What if one option led to total vehicular destruction? What if there was only enough road to gain the momentum to get you to the top of an even higher hill? How was a girl to know?

Los Angeles is a city of people who want to see their names in lights. I was starting with slightly lower expectations—like, um, my own cubicle.

San Francisco is known for having lots of jobs in advertising. But it also requires so much damn walking. The only exercise I'd had in years was walking between bars on Sixth Street in Austin.

New York City wouldn't work. Too many people, all who had more of everything than I did. More money, more style, more ambition for both of those things. My highest hope was that one day I would manage to leave my house without white deodorant streaks on my dress from Old Navy. No, I definitely was not ready to show my wardrobe in Soho.

Eventually I got overwhelmed with picking a city to start fresh in and so I decided to search for a decision that I could handle. I went on the search for a new haircut. Chopping five inches off my hair was my usual go-to solution for breaking points in life, but in the past I'd only utilized the technique for breakups with boyfriends. The rationale? If you're insides are chopped up to messy, raw pieces, why not have your outsides look the same way. I was about to take a picture of Meg Ryan to my hairdresser with instructions to *"make me look like her"* (which would have been a challenge since Meg is a size two and I was a size more reflective of the PTSD I was suffering: Post Traumatic Sorority Disorder) when my phone rang. On the other end of the line was a friend from my advertising program in college, she'd gotten an internship in Boston and was sure there were plenty more to be had in the city.

"Had I ever been to Boston?" No. "Did I have an opinion one way or another about the city?" Not really. I knew they had a lot of fish and chips, which was good thing, I couldn't move anywhere that didn't pay due respect to fried foods. "Would I consider moving there?" As long as there were no overly stylish people who would mock me for my deodorant stains. She assured me that no one in Boston had any style whatsoever and so I told her I'd consider it.

I did more than consider the move. I got in my car, drove to the bookstore, and bought every guidebook I could find on Boston. I read about historical halls, marathons, Harvard. I imagined myself soaking up Americana, cheering on the Kenyan runners, teaching a Harvard man the many joys of a Tex-Mex margarita while he whispered sweet algorithms in my ear.

I was in. Sight unseen. Boston accent unheard. It would be the farthest north any person in my family had ever lived.

The decision was made so fast it was like I'd spent six months saving up to go on a vacation. Tahiti or London? Beach or urban area? And then one day I get some spam in my in-box toting the joys of Africa and the next thing you know I'm spending every dollar I have to take a safari through the jungle and cheer on random wildebeest sex.

Not necessarily a bad decision, just a wholly unexpected one. Especially since the control freak in me loathes spontaneity with the venom of two women fighting over the same man. In a country bar. With Budweiser in their blood streams. And both of them with children of his back in their respective homes. The upshot was that Boston might kick my ass, but I'd be moving in with my college friend, so at least I wouldn't get beat up alone.

I didn't waste money on a visit to Boston first to make sure it was the right choice. Instead, I packed my bags, bought a plane ticket, and we moved into an apartment my friend found online.

Neither of us had ever lived in a city that had basements, much less basement apartments. So even though I say we moved into an apartment, it was more like moving into a cave that only saw sunlight when we trapped the rays in mason jars and brought them inside with us. She got a boyfriend to keep her life cheery, and I

CALL ME A PARTNER IN COHABITATION CRIME

decided to get busy with finding a way to adjust to Boston. It felt like I'd simply woken up one morning in a brand-new city—and of course that was exactly what had happened. The tricky part was I felt like I should have a brand new life to match. And that required a serious undertaking to rid myself of some of my previously unquestioned Southern ways. If my fall from grace is the climax of my life in Boston, then my first six months would be the series of inevitable events that were steps to the edge of the cliff I'd eventually tumble from.

I stopped saying y'all. Until I had more than one beer in me and then my mouth ran on automatic pilot.

I let the tan I'd been proud of for years fade to the milky pale pallor of a sophisticated urban dweller. I just pretended all my freckles were a natural part of my complexion, and not the result of a serious lack of SPF in my youth.

The pastel T-shirts so appropriate in the South were slowly replaced with black sweaters. Lots and lots of black sweaters. Enough black sweaters that one might wonder whether I was trying to transform my closet into a place where Marilyn Manson would feel at home.

I learned how to take the T without holding onto the rails for dear life every time the train came to a halt.

And how to maneuver in the crowds at Fenway without ending up in the hospital (Don't wear a Yankees jersey and never, ever cut in the beer line.)

I found out that bars were good places for actual conversation. Previously I'd believed them to only be useful as backup venues to frat houses for getting drunk enough to stomach listening to what frat boys had to say.

I settled into an internship where I mostly made coffee but eventually was allowed to serve that coffee to more senior copywriters who let me watch over their shoulders. And then finally I landed a full-time job where I still made coffee but was also given control of a keyboard on occasion.

And perhaps most important, I realized that work was not so bad. And actually kind of fun. A hell of a lot more fun than I'd grown up thinking it would be. My freedom didn't feel crunched by my cubicle—after all, someone was giving me money and health insurance in exchange for my time spent there. The girls who'd married after college for those same securities couldn't walk away from their husbands at five o'clock. And regardless of how one feels about working for The Man, or The Man's Man, or The Man's third cousin (who is probably also a man), it's really nice to pay the rent without selling organs which, though seemingly useless now, you may very well end up needing someday.

One day, instead of waking up and feeling like I was lost in a new city, I woke up, looked around, and saw that all the important details of my life had been completely transformed by my move to Boston; I'd slid into a self that was not even related to the fearful girl who'd graduated from college months before. And this new self wore her new style—which showed fewer and fewer deodorant marks—with confidence.

But one hurdle remained in my quest to establish a brand-new life: I still had never had a relationship with a man who wasn't Southern.

This realization occurred about the same time the holiday season arrived. The snow was cold, but all the free booze that the advertising industry was throwing around town warmed my heart. It was at one of these industry holiday parties when just what I had been waiting for walked up to the bar and ordered a drink.

He was missing the beer belly I knew so well from fraternity guys in Texas.

And the pleated khaki pants.

And daddy's credit card. How much more advanced! To be drinking on a corporate credit card!

CALL ME A PARTNER IN COHABITATION CRIME

As nonchalantly as I could, I visually examined his nether region for a belt buckle that obnoxiously announced his name. There was none that I could see.

Southern girls could have their Prince Charmings on horse-back, I'd found my Yankee.

Try not to be weird, I reminded myself. *Try not to be weird.* And I walked up next to him at the bar and smiled.

He looked at me for one beat, and then, in the moment he should have been seduced by my Southern charm, he turned and walked away.

Apparently dating in the real world wasn't as easy as getting drunk and exchanging flirtatious looks until you became an official couple who got drunk and exchanged fraternity and sorority T-shirts.

Luckily for me, the advertising industry in Boston is not only well connected, it's also rather incestuous. I worked with people who knew people who worked with him and over the first few weeks of the New Year my number was passed his way. In a move that I thought was auspicious at the time, he called me on Valentine's Day (until I decided Valentine's Day was a bullshit holiday, which, now that we aren't together, actually keeps his call auspicious for having happened on that day) and asked me on a (not really) blind (because I'd already seen him) date.

I'd had two months to build a story of his northeastern perfection in my mind. The way he would never open doors for me. How he would pronounce his vowels the way God intended instead of slurring them into a verbal cauldron of mess-hall slop. General ignorance in any conversation on NASCAR. When he finally arrived at my apartment to pick me up for a date, the story was solidified and my heart officially opened—there was no pickup truck, no SUV that could manage any ranch terrain; he arrived in a sensibly small Volkswagen that might even be described by some as cute. I'd never known a man behind the wheel of such a small vehicle, and so I knew he was the antithesis to the Southern man. In other words, he was perfect.

The date went well, and so did the one after that and the two after that. I cooked him a Southern meal and while under the spell of cornbread, he declared I was his girlfriend. He claimed he hadn't seen me that first night at the holiday party. I claimed it didn't bother me because he noticed me now. After a couple months passed and I was secure that the relationship was solid, I called different friends at home to announce that my Boston life was complete.

They'd been waiting on this call for months. I'd phone my friends to report that I'd finally moved from an internship to a full-time job or how I was totally positive that I'd discovered the next Tracy Chapman in Harvard Square, but all they cared about was which guy was the cutest in my office and was I dating him. When there was no guy in the picture, I heard crickets in the phone.

"You there?" I'd ask.

"Oh yes, yes," they'd say, "Were you saying something about a Chacy Trapman?"

Finally I had news they could sink their teeth into. But instead of being excited for me, they just had more questions. Would I bring him home to meet my parents? Did I think he was The One I would spend my life with? They were just concerned about my well-being. After all, in their eyes time was running out. If I didn't have a ring by twenty-two then it would be difficult to get mini-vanned by twenty-five.

But I had just gotten settled in Boston. I wanted more exotic experiences, like pad thai noodles and strangers who would cuss each other out in the streets. I'd never met people who were Irish more than one day a year and now I lived in a place where the pubs were packed with them. I wasn't thinking marriage; I was wondering what word he'd used his whole life in place of y'all.

Three months.

CALL ME A PARTNER IN COHABITATION CRIME

Six months.

Nine months passed.

My friends were tapping their fingernails on the phone, waiting to see where this relationship was going.

Disney princesses and romantic comedies had planted the seed long ago in my brain, but in the excitement of my new Boston life I'd managed to ignore it. Now my friends were practically dumping water into the soil and the seed was starting to sprout. But I didn't want it to grow into an everyday plant, perfectly manicured like shrubs lining a white picket fence. I wanted something different. I didn't want to shoot for marriage, but I wanted the security of commitment.

I hated myself for it, but I heard the impatience of my friends and I started to wonder what I was going to do with this mangy plant he and I had growing in every direction. I wanted to ask where he saw us going, and I wanted him to answer in a way that would cut the weeds back and let us continue to grow.

And so I planned the conversation. I thought it through. I decided I would wait until neither of us was stressed with work, nor in bed. I knew both situations tended to yield not-true opinions and answers.

Then I did what I always do after I have carefully planned out a life-changing conversation. I had a glass of wine and brought up the question in a completely impromptu and disorganized way.

And though the conversation is mildly foggy, when I escaped the haze of my hangover I had vague memories of the ideas we exchanged.

Marriage was out of the question. For both of us. We were too young, and what was the rush? Why not live a little, move around some. He mentioned wanting to see the West Coast. I believe I made some inarticulate comments about how it would be like, so rad, to live the West Coast-surfer lifestyle.

We ordered another round of drinks. Mine might have been a double.

He had lots of friends who lived together before they got married, and their success made it seem like a good idea to him.

I had zero friends who had lived together, which made it seem like a good idea to me.

We could commit to each other without sliding rings on fingers.

I'd have the security I wanted, but in a brand-new way.

We could play house. Which was kind of like playing life in Boston—and I'd had success at that game.

Of course, living with a man was an entirely new concept—not something I'd ever envisioned for myself. But the longer I sat with the idea, the more it made sense to my brain that was newly seasoned with more liberated ways of living. Getting married because it was what our parents and all those people in the Old Testament did seemed foolish. I'd bounce the idea of young marriage off people I knew in Boston and they would nod their heads in agreement and join me in loud laughter. "It's just so archaic!" we'd exclaim between hoots and hollers.

And then I would ponder my boyfriend's more "enlightened" friends who were sharing leases before vows, bathrooms before honeymoons. Their relationships did have a certain worldliness and independence, as well as an excitement, I'd never attached to my friends who married early and immediately settled into a groove they'd stay in until death did them part.

Pretty soon the whole living together arrangement started to sound good. Obviously I was already lagging behind in the race for weddings, mortgages, and minivans, so why not sign up for a different race. Not a consolation bracket, but a race that had another set of rules—an altogether separate competition. I hadn't given up on the idea that I would eventually end up in the same place as those people who sprinted out of the gates. But like a

CALL ME A PARTNER IN COHABITATION CRIME

marathon runner who says to hell with it and jumps on the subway so she can get a burger and some beer before rejoining the pack at the end of the mileage, I'd find my own way to the finish line.

I thought I was buying a ticket to a town called An Even Better Deal than Marriage-ville. In my mind this town was built on a commitment that transcended convention, sharing the nuances of everyday life before you vowed to share forever, and also the occasional breakfast in bed with orange juice, fresh scones, and *The New York Times* that isn't possible once children are in the picture.

My grandma had given me the Silent Treatment as warning that perhaps I was heading to a town I didn't quite know how to pack a suitcase for. But I was busy exploring and thought I was charting new territory that no one in my life had the right experience to guide me through. That was why I eventually chose to move forward with the move in and wait for her to catch up. I was not going to heed her warning because I thought I was paving a brand-new way.

But in the end I should have heeded her warning, because my ticket was to a different town than I planned on moving to. When I actually looked down at the stub in my hand I found I was headed for Too Close for Comfort Without Breaks for Federal Taxes or Non-Monogamous Sex-ville. The doors were already closed. Seat belts fastened. All the luggage had been stowed. It was like getting on a plane you thought was bound for Los Angeles, and then discovering you will actually be landing in Scranton.

This is where reality should be suspended for a moment. And not by any pansy-ass suspenders, no, sirree, a pair of those weaklings would not do this trick . The reality we are holding back is so heavy with baggage it requires a couple steel cables, maybe a Mack Truck to pick up the remains and drive them far, far away.

The sad fact of the matter is that my domestic partnership was not pretty. The arrangement was like being attracted to someone in a bar and then, as your beer buzz wears off, realizing whatever attraction you'd felt had worn off as well. Full of fun in the beginning, by the end of the night you're practically begging the waitress for your check so you can get the hell out of there. Except imagine that deterioration happening over the course of years.

Happily, all parties involved moved on and up. And the man I lived with held no more blame than I did for what was fundamentally wrong in the relationship. But because I am the one behind the keyboard, I have the power to make it seem that way. Being that I am a spiteful, spiteful woman—the kind of woman who wishes secret servings of whole milk on all the skinny girls I see at Starbucks—I will remove the temptation to create him as an evil-doing character by taking out the "he did this" and "he fucked that ups" from my tale of domestic partnership so that my telling is more about the nuts and bolts of two romantically involved human beings living in the same shared quarters and less about shining a flashlight into the dark, back corners of my own personal closet.

Because out of the Southern acquaintances and friends, strangers eavesdropping at restaurants, and my dear grandmother—all of whom I knew disapproved of me living with a man—no one gave me the speech that might actually have given me pause. There were lots of raised eyebrows and weeks of the Silent Treatment, but very few words of actual warning. I can't say what my reaction would have been if anyone had spoken of their concerns. Would I have changed my course? Reconsidered the decision? It's doubtful.

All I know is that no one gave me the hard and gritty preview of a trip through the town of Too Close for Comfort Without Breaks for Federal Taxes or Non-Monogamous Sex-ville and broke down how I could expect life there to really be. I thought we were going to play house, but in reality we were entering territory that neither of us had played in before. Would we have traveled to Cambodia

CALL ME A PARTNER IN COHABITATION CRIME

sans tour guides and guarantees that we could emerge safely? Never. But a 1 Bdrm w/study apartment seemed controllable and safe. We could never be hurt there like we would be if a tribe of rebels were unleashed into our Cambodian hostel. Right? Only in hindsight can I say we were probably wrong.

You know when you've entered TCC-ville (as Too Close for Comfort Without Breaks for Federal Taxes or Non-Monogamous Sex-ville shall be known from here on out) because you immediately pass the population sign. TWO, it says. This isn't a wishy-washy two. Like, a two that could be six if a few friends come and crash for the weekend. Or, a two that goes down to one if someone leaves for a work trip. This two never changes. In the middle of a crowded cocktail party, at a relative's fourteen-person holiday dinner, from here on out, you are a town of two within any number of people you stand in.

With a population of two, you might make a mistake and think we aren't talking about a real town. But we are. Trust me, we are. Only two people live here, but between those two there is enough commerce, enterprise, and local politics to be a viable point on any map.

Right past the population sign is the town gas station. It looks desolate on the outside, but that's only because the pumps are rusty—this station doesn't offer gas for cars. Peer inside and you'll see the fuel that keeps a couple going. Snickers, Twizzlers, extra-large servings of Mountain Dew and coffee so strong and thick the cream puddles on top instead of mixing with the liquid. Every item that helps a couple through those long nights when one partner has been kicked out of the bed and must pass the time until the no-fly zone in the bedroom has been lifted.

No one works the checkout counter at the gas station. This is the case at every store in town. An honor system is used for all transactions in TCC-ville—every town member is responsible for putting in what they take out. If someone is consistently taking more Twizzlers than they restock after a trip to the grocery store, it could be indicative of a much larger problem. Are they also incurring emotional debts that they have no intention of replenishing?

Drive on from the gas station and a person comes to the only intersection in town. If you're all fueled up on the green caffeine—in other words, if you're doing The Dew—and feeling courageous then it's a good day to turn right. Turning right requires forethought and patience (and if chocolate chip cookies give you the same comfort they give to me then maybe pack a baker's dozen) because once you turn right you are on a road that has one destination: the town cemetery.

This cemetery doesn't hold bodies of people who have lived in town; there are no corpses in the ground. Instead, what's buried here are stories, feelings, and memories of old relationships put to rest. A summertime snapshot with the one who got away, or some Match.com emails mulching into the earth.

People who live in town visit the cemetery when they are feeling dissatisfied with their current roommate. Those who enter alone have likely been engaging in behavior that amplifies this dissatisfaction. A solitary hit off a joint has led them to this contemplative juncture, or maybe just staring too long at the endless pile of laundry their current live-in leaves on the floor. This person is looking for a nostalgic escape from the claustrophobia of their current situation—even if it is only a temporary leave from the reservation.

When a person brings their partner with them into the cemetery, it is usually an attempt to communicate expectations that aren't being met now, but have been met by others in their past.

For example, a mixtape of UB40 that was played during college hook-up sessions might remind a townsperson of a time when lots and lots of attention was paid to her vagina. By taking a current boyfriend to the grave where that tape is buried, this person might

CALL ME A PARTNER IN COHABITATION CRIME

be communicating that her vagina is feeling ignored, perhaps even listless or a little bit lonely.

Whether with a partner or alone, should someone stumble into an especially deep grave, say with memorabilia from a very first love, the only way up is to think about times the two townspeople have been very happy together: holding hands when neither got too sweaty, or when a bottle of wine and a movie left them thinking they could have their very own happy ending.

Finding the good is what gets a cemetery visitor back on the main road—heading away from the past and toward what is hopefully a happier future.

It can take just moments to get from the cemetery to the home, or from the home to the gas station—traditional modes of transportation aren't required in this town. And so traffic laws are irrelevant. In fact, laws of physics don't even apply. A townsperson might be sitting at a breakfast table, minding his own business with a bowl of Honey Nut Cheerios, when out of the blue the other townsperson barges into the kitchen and immediately transports them into the bottom of Plot 436 at the town cemetery. Plot 436 is where a picture of her boyfriend from two years previous resides. The boyfriend from Pensacola. Who always waited to start breakfast until she was at the table so they could eat their Honey Nut Cheerios in a blissful state of codependent togetherness.

But one can use this quick movement to go any place in town—not just the cemetery. And there are so many more locations in town to enjoy (thankfully!).

If you were to take a left at the crossroads where going right led you to the cemetery, you will end up at the home base—one might say, the heart—of town. This is not the downtown (we'll get to that), but rather where the most important business gets done. The sex, the screaming, the softly whispered apologies. These activities occur in the beating aorta of the relationship—the home space that is shared.

Much like the neighborhood haunted house, which everyone knows how it looks on the outside but can only have an opinion on what happens inside, only those who reside there really have the true story of what it's like to live there.

Standard visitors like pizza deliverymen, old college friends who arrive with suitcases in tow, and great Aunt Linda(s) may cross the threshold for a time, but that doesn't grant access to the full picture. Only the two permanent residents know the giggling, the plate-throwing, the nights spent wondering if they've stayed in town for too long—perhaps pondering if it's time to tie the knot and go for the federal tax breaks, or maybe if they should go their separate ways since each of them is already having non-monogamous sex with residents of the next town over.

For a shortcut from the residence to downtown, cut through the backyard. As you walk through the yard you might note any debris lying around. A well-maintained tomato garden is a good sign that the relationship is thriving. The contents of an underwear drawer lying under a Hummingbird feeder with the actual drawer discarded nearby—not as encouraging.

The first downtown building you'll come upon is the library. This isn't the library of your elementary school years. First of all, books only take up a portion of shelf space. Alongside the books are bottles of detergent, blenders, some greeting cards, and a constantly refilled drawer of stamps. Anything and everything that one town resident borrows from another resident is here. If a resident needs five dollars to pick up dry cleaning but doesn't have any cash, the resident is more than welcome to the other resident's five-dollar bill that is in the library shelves. But if the five-dollar bill is not paid back in a timely manner, that could require a trip to the bank.

Conveniently, the bank is located next to the library. But this is not bank business as usual—there isn't a friendly greeter waiting at the front door, there aren't a slew of banking assistants ready to

CALL ME A PARTNER IN COHABITATION CRIME

sign a person up for a "free" checking account. This establishment is actually two different banks run by two presidents (the two residents of town) who often have different agendas (one might be interested in saving for a house in Marriage-ville, while the other is craving a tequila-fueled romp through Cancun) and management styles (one likes to stay on top of banking issues and the other lets them pile up until creditors start calling).

These two management styles are not the fault of either banker. You can't blame a person for growing up with a mother who believed in material things more than maternal instincts anymore than you can blame someone for being a nickel-watcher. But at the end of the day, these are the differences that keep this particular bank in a constant state of flux. Money makes the world go round, yes, but it is also occasionally responsible for the stability of this town swirling straight down the shitter.

There is a break from the tension of banking transactions. The bank in TCC-ville closes on all federally recognized holidays, as well as the local ones, which include but are not limited to birthdays, anniversaries, planned occasions to try new sex toys, and any time one resident decides to shop for shoes at Nordies.

There is space in the downtown area for loafing about. A picnic area is blocked off for the occasional Sunday afternoon meal or romp in the grass (the kind of afternoon that is the only acceptable reason to play James Taylor tunes—ever—if you're under age forty). Because there are only two residents in town, outdoor sex doesn't run the risk of offending families who like to keep their lives rated PG or the single passersby who might become offended because they are in the middle of an especially dry spell.

A podium is set up in this space for the occasional speech that affects public policy. This speaking area is directly across from the bank, because often a town resident will need the formality of the podium to deliver a position on town finance. For example, whether someone should be able to take a loan from the shared savings account for a new iPhone.

In addition to money talks, residents speak at the podium when they need to establish boundaries on how often in-laws can visit, whether friendships with exes are tolerated, pancakes versus waffles for Sunday brunch, and the oft-debatable topic of whether watching television in nothing but underwear and a pair of socks is intolerable or endearing.

Politics are alive and well in this town. A mayor (again, one of the two residents) is always presiding over order, but the identity of that mayor has been known to shift as many times as there are minutes in a day. Doing the laundry can give one control of the town key, just as bringing home fresh flowers, cleaning the bathroom, and not being the one who drinks twelve beers with buddies and then forgets to call home can also guarantee a power shift. Being mayor simply means that you have the final say in all matters of the hour. If you subscribe to Clintonian-style politics, it also means you get the lead sound bite that's featured in that day's town newspaper.

So, we've covered the gas station, the cemetery, the main residence, the library, the bank, and the outdoor town center. The last stop before getting to the edge of town is the town bar. The town bar is always dark. The town bar never closes. And the only liquor that the town bar serves is whiskey. The town bar is never a destination, it is a place that residents accidentally stumble into when they are too drunk to know it's time to go straight home for bed. The town bar is a place where catastrophic wars have started, a place that often serves as a transporter pad for visits to the cemetery, a place where people occasionally fall asleep on a bar stool instead of going in their own bed. The town bar is located near the edge of town because, for many, it is the final stop before they give a final goodbye to living in sin.

Of course, there are some people who never leave TCC-ville. They move in, unpack their boxes, stretch their legs, and decide they like the feeling of that town.

But if the residents should decide they are ready to blow out of town after a few weeks or maybe months, they have a couple options as to which highway they should take.

If the town has been a place to hang out for a couple years while people assure themselves they are ready for the next step—like spending a couple years at a community college before you step up to a university—then the first highway is actually a long aisle. Usually carpeted, but in the case of a destination wedding to Mexico or the Caribbean, it could also be made of sand. At the end of that highway/aisle is a priest and a smattering of close friends, all wearing the same style of dresses and suits they wore to their senior proms. Following a crescendo of orchestra music, the bride walks down the aisle and meets her wedding posse, as well as her future husband. There are flowers that smell really nice and people who throw rice. If you believe everything you've ever heard from the folks at Baylor University, this is the only road that will lead to happiness.

The other highway that heads out of town is actually one that splits into two roads with each townsperson heading a different way. When a person leaves TCC-ville on their own, it can be difficult to keep the ole chin up. After all, you are used to being part of a team, a serving of peanut butter to another person's jelly, a receiver to their quarterback, the Guinness to half a pint of Bass. The easiest way to deal with a solo departure is with a to-go cup from the town bar and lots of positive thoughts. There are plenty of times when being alone is much better than being half of two—in a twin bed, for example, or when you really want to keep the second Twix bar for yourself.

An important thing to remember before a person takes this route out of town is that even though it may seem easier to leave the details for later, there will be regret if one does not claim each and every one of their belongings. Maybe months of fighting over the role of religion in the relationship makes bickering over a blink-182 CD feel frivolous, but believe you me, in two years you are going to be sitting in your brand-new room in a brand-new town and it is going to occur to you that nothing in the world would sound better than some California-teen rocker angst. And even though it seems like a disappointment it's actually a larger victory because at this moment, not having that CD will truly be your only regret.

Eventually you'll forget what it was like to sleep with the person.

You'll get over the cute way the other person used to get the hiccups when they were stressed (and with luck, you will realize how annoying that actually was).

I exited TCC-ville without my significant other in tow. My exit was so abrupt and quick I didn't even get to stop at the town bar on the way out. I have personal experience with blink-182 CDs that get forgotten in the fray. The one I was ashamed to love was, quite unfortunately, gone forever.

There were people, surely, who believed that they "had told me so." But I do know that my grandmother is not one of them. Sure, she wishes I had not provided reason to deliver the Silent Treatment to her beloved granddaughter. But she saw that the silence I endured when he moved out was almost more than anyone who truly loved me could stomach.

For so damn long I wanted to believe that I was a grown-up because I had moved to the other side of the country alone, or because I was doing something different than my friends from college, or because I was choosing to share a bed with a man out of matrimony. My brain said these three big decisions all added together should equal one adult woman.

CALL ME A PARTNER IN COHABITATION CRIME

But I couldn't force being a grown-up, no matter how hard I tried. I could put all the pieces of the grown-up puzzle in order, but until the right glue was inside me, none of those pieces were going to stick.

When I was living in TCC-ville, my grandma and I didn't talk about my roommate too much. We'd talk about the weather and new recipes, so when my living situation changed our topics of conversation stayed about the same.

And that was all fine and well because no one could give me a short cut around the highway out of town. I would stop for days or weeks at a rest stop. I'd pitch a tent if I got tired. It was nice to pick up the phone and have a friendly voice on the other end of the line, but making it to the end of that road was something I had to do for myself.

In the end I made it to a new town, and by the time I got there I was overjoyed to find a population of one. There was nowhere I needed to journey to or leave. I could just be my own destination for a while. I kept my black sweaters, but I reintroduced some of the pastel T-shirts back into my wardrobe, too. I took back my y'all, but never went back to a full-on drawl. I still have love for public transportation. I'm a little older, (possibly) a little wiser, and (gladly) a little too cynical to try on new lives like they are skirts in a dressing room. I appreciate the value in a hallelujah when an upside-down cake comes out of the oven without going downside up.

And finally, I decided that I'd spent enough time in my own relationship cemetery that I was ready to padlock the outside gate and start with a fresh plot of land.

Chapter 7

Call Me A Squatter

I didn't fall in love with New York City from the top of the Empire State Building or the first time I sat on a bench in Central Park. *Sex and the City* didn't give me my starry-eyed view of Manhattan from the vantage point of six-inch stilettos. I can't even blame my affection on a vacation to New York City as a youth. My family only traveled places we could drive to in our van. And because we had to reach those places before my father's patience disappeared, South Carolina was as far north as we ever ventured.

My love story with New York isn't a romantic one, because it was an acquired affection. Like realizing you have a crush on a coworker after you've sat in meetings with him five days a week for two years. I fell in love with Manhattan from staring day after day and night after night at a mural that came along with the bedroom of the house we moved into when I was in the first grade.

That summer before first grade my family moved Louisiana to Houston. Changing cities wasn't especially monumental. We moved frequently while I was growing up, and were accustomed to putting our lives in boxes and then unpacking them in a new zip code, most times a new state. When people hear how much I moved around, they usually ask if I was an army brat. I tell them that my father worked in refineries—the brattiness was an extra bonus I managed to develop without the help of the U.S. armed forces.

But this particular move was difficult. In Louisiana I went to a private school and was required to wear a uniform, which seriously impaired my ability to spend every waking second in my favorite MENUDO T-shirt. Nothing in Louisiana looked like my old life in Houston—fewer malls, and more grassy moss. My mom and I could drive around town all day without ever getting on a highway. I missed the way our car used to race alongside other drivers on the roads. I missed the friends I'd left behind.

I asked my parents if we could move back to Texas and the answer was that I should go outside and play.

"Outside in Texas?" I'd ask.

"Outside here, where we live now," my mom would say.

I'd go to my bedroom and lay down with the lights off. The opposite of playing. I likely thought I was making a point. Really I was just making myself miserable.

During those long afternoons, just enough sunlight made it through the curtains so I could see the wall that faced my bed. And this wall wasn't covered with posters or paint. It was a floor-to-ceiling wallpaper that pictured an aerial photograph of downtown New York City.

When we first moved in, my parents had made a list of things that needed to be changed. The photographic mural was on the list, but considering the kitchen was papered in a fluorescent fruitopia, my bedroom wasn't the top priority.

So for those first two months, while I was trying to adjust to a new school and a new town and the distressing fact that I was only in the first grade but life already seemed to have gone very wrong, I found New York City waiting for me when I retreated to my room.

I'd stare at that wall and think, *Why on earth would a city need so many buildings?* I'd wonder where they found enough people to live in all of them.

Then I'd pull my bedspread up so I was tightly cocooned and wonder whether I'd grow up and go live in one of those buildings.

The stories I made up about life in New York City were typical for a young girl. There I was in my MENUDO T-shirt on the top floor of a skyscraper, working in an office. Or down in the streets between the tall buildings wearing my MENUDO T-shirt and kissing a man who was my boyfriend, who looked conspicuously similar to John Travolta.

When I moved to New York City as an adult, I would sometimes think about the mural. I'd walk up the avenues, across the streets, through the crowds, and I'd wonder if the person who'd slept in that room before me was on the island with me now, too. You'd have to love a city a whole lot to paste it across your bedroom wall. I imagined after so many years of loving a place like that, it was inevitable that a person would have to go live there.

After all, that was exactly how it happened for me.

The only thing that made me different at my school in Louisiana was the fact that I was the new kid in town. I decided I needed another something to make me unique, and so I started to tell anyone who'd listen how much I liked New York City. Someone would

CALL ME A SQUATTER

ask me if I liked living in Louisiana and I'd say that I didn't mind it so much, but I imagined that New York City would be better.

If an adult wanted to know what I planned to be when I grew up, I'd say, "Any kind of job as long as it's in New York City."

If we had a paper to write for geography class I'd choose New York City. If someone else had already chosen it then I'd take neighboring New Jersey. But I'd be pissed about it. (Not that I was allowed to be "pissed off" at my private school. We'll say I was "piously peeved.")

Of course, my love for New York ebbed and flowed. Other things came up in my life, like boys, hormones, and the occasional pimple that needed constant vigilance with makeup borrowed from my mother. But the fantasy of living in New York City was too strong to disappear for long; it always bubbled back to the surface.

And so when the time came to decide where I wanted to move after college, my family assumed I'd pack my bags for New York. When I said I wasn't so sure that was the right choice, my parents looked at me as though they wanted a fingerprint ID to verify that I was, in fact, the same person who had lived under their roof for seventeen years.

They asked why I'd changed my mind and I made an excuse about the fast-paced lifestyle. I said I probably wouldn't get a job that paid enough for rent, not to mention how difficult it would be to obtain clothes that wouldn't cause people on the street to fall down in hysterics. Being out of fashion in New York City could put you out of a social group faster than sleeping on park benches.

My mom still looked as though she thought her real daughter might return whenever the aliens dropped her our of their spaceship and took back this temporary-replacement person. But neither she nor my dad argued with me. I appreciated that, considering it was my own major life decision to fuck up as I pleased.

Deep down, I knew that I'd given good reasons for not trying it out, but none were the real reason. For so long New York City

JUST DON'T CALL ME MA'AM

had been the perfect place for me to live. If I moved there and life wasn't perfect, then where would I have to go?

And so I stayed away. I moved to a city I knew nothing about, which allowed me to blame plenty of problems on it.

It took three and a half years of life-after-college for me to jump my hurdle of fear and move to New York City. And even then, I didn't leap because I believed I could land on my own two feet. I was jumping with the Yankee, so I'd have a safety net in case of an imperfect landing. We'd already been living together for about a year and a half after moving from Boston to Seattle. Both of us had always wanted to live in New York but had never wanted to do it alone.

We would get an apartment in Brooklyn.

We would finally find the love we kept searching for—in cities, and furniture stores, and anywhere domestic bliss was rumored to be sold.

Life would be perfect.

We got the apartment in Brooklyn. But the love thing didn't go as planned and life ended up less than perfect. The breakup that ensued after just a few months in this new place scrambled my life so bad it was like trying to decipher a conversation at the ungodly (but very New Yorker) hour of four o'clock in the morning.

Unfortunately, it took more than a few public displays of sadness (a person might think sunglasses are rarely needed underground, but that person has never been caught with the urge to cry furiously on a subway) and many, many moons (not just individual moons, we're talking full lunar cycles). But I eventually got my head and my life back together. The first order of business was to leave the apartment he and I had shared. And the choice was mine to either remain somewhere in New York City, or to go.

I decided that leaving was not an option. I'd had dreams of living there since I'd been a little girl in Louisiana. I signed a lease

CALL ME A SQUATTER

on a space that the realtor claimed as an apartment, but was really more the size of a bocce ball court.

The upside was that I could sit on my bed and toss trash into the bathroom trash can on the opposite side of the apartment. The downside was that I could only fit a dorm-sized refrigerator in the kitchen. But I'll be damned if it was my very own rectangle of space in Manhattan.

I got new clothes. New furniture. A new job that provided new friends. Convenient since lots of mine were casualties of the break-up. My apartment was on the fifth floor of a walk-up building, so I estimated that after living there for two months I would have a brand-new set of calf muscles, and, if I was lucky, a new and improved ass.

I started checking boxes and I didn't stop until my life looked exactly like I imagined the life of a single girl in Manhattan should look. I went to work every day in the middle of the tall buildings and on the weekends I shopped with friends. Occasionally, I had the opportunity to kiss a man on a city street. I'd kick back my right heel in the middle of it, just for shits and giggles, just because I imagined this wasn't something girls back home would do.

Minus one MENUDO T-shirt, I had taken every step I could to turn my childhood fantasy of New York City into reality. Except I'd forgotten the cardinal rule in having fantasies: Confuse them with reality and they'll melt away faster than an ice sculpture in July. And eventually my experiment with building my very own fairy tale did come to an end.

There was no fairy-tale glamour in this ending. I didn't lose a glass slipper or hear the clock chime midnight as I ran down the steps of a grand staircase. My ending was delivered via a conversation with the head of the human resources department at my new job. No frog turning into a prince, zero breathtaking sunsets.

He was balding, and throughout the conversation he rubbed his stomach as though he were suffering from indigestion.

The advertising agency where I worked had lost their biggest client. And so I was losing my job.

I understood that this was just part of the advertising game, didn't I?

I wasn't going to cry, was I?

Yes, I understood. No, I wasn't going to cry. But I was seriously considering hurling a chair through the window onto the street. And then jumping out behind it.

When I returned to my desk, I started to pack my things along with the other eighty people who would also be leaving the office that day for the last time. I sat on the box of belongings I was taking with me and ate the final bites of the yogurt parfait that I'd deserted when I saw Mr. Human Resources heading my way. I had a strong suspicion that over-priced, organic breakfast delights were about to become a thing of the past; especially now that I would be without health insurance, there was no reason to let the valuable nutrition in that granola go to waste.

I took the long route home even though I was carrying my box of belongings. Every few blocks I would stop to rest and wonder how the hell this had happened to me. Other people got laid off. People who worked in factories and plants, places that had thousands of employees and were susceptible to business moving overseas to an Asian country, or maybe a call center in India. I had gone to college. I had gotten a degree. I had gotten dumped the year before. I had paid my dues, damn it.

To say Lady Luck wasn't looking my way was a delicate way to describe the situation: she'd downright snubbed me.

The first people I called when I got home were my parents. And my father summed up the situation with all the eloquence of his East Texas roots.

"Might be time for you to flush, girl," he said. "Seems to me everything's in the shitter."

Comforting, he wasn't. But he was correct. I'd done my best to play the part of a New York City gal. I'd built the set, bought the props, and even learned to go through the motions—hell, I could run after a cab while wearing high heels *and* text messaging on my cell phone.

But the quality of the performance I gave didn't matter, the script kept returning to the same end. New York was the perfect city, but my life there was anything but perfect. First, love had crashed. Then work had followed suit.

I had to decide if I wanted to stand up, dust myself off, and soldier on. But for all the soldiering I'd done when I left the apartment in Brooklyn—in and out of my office day after day, in and out of subways and crowds and the chaos on the streets—I felt like I was soldiering through every damn day without gaining any real ground.

And so I seriously started to consider leaving the one city I'd always thought I would be able to love above all others.

(One helpful hint for people who embark on a soul-searching journey that involves lots of flinging yourself dramatically on the sofa while you ponder the meaning of life: Be sure your apartment has enough space to fit a sofa.)

For three days I curled on my love seat and teetered on the edge of a decision. Every fiber of my body wanted to leave but my brain kept telling me to stick it out, to try and make Manhattan work. It was just a job, I told myself, there would be others.

But I would be stepping up to bat with two strikes, and I had a sneaking suspicion that the more I tried to force the city to work with me, the more I was forcing my third strike. I didn't want to be thrown out. I wanted to leave on my own terms.

I called my parents again and my mother answered the phone.

"I'm thinking of coming home," I said.

"Okay," my mom said. "Some time away would probably be a good thing."

"Well," I said, "I'm thinking about bringing some of my things with me when I come home."

"It's best that you bring some things, honey, people here are rabid Baptists, not nudists."

"More than clothes, Mom," I said. "I'm thinking of bringing all my things and moving back home."

There was a long silence during which I realized I'd assumed my parents would want me back, that they would welcome me with open arms.

"Moving into our home?" she asked.

"Yes," I said.

"You do remember that our home is in the South," she said.

"Yes," I said.

"And so coming to stay here would mean you living in the South again," she said.

"Yes," I answered. "But it might just be a brief period of time. I'm thinking one month, maybe two."

"But you do remember that conversation we've had about eight hundred times since you left the South, the conversation where I ask if you are ever going to live in the South again and you say that you would consider it if and only if the north was destroyed in some sort of nuclear attack," she said.

"Yes," I said. "I remember that conversation."

"So did I miss something important in the news?" she asked.

I took a deep breath.

"Let's just say I'm reconsidering my previous position," I answered.

"Hmph," she said. And she sat there. "You know, I'm not sure that's good enough."

It was my turn to be silent. I told her I would talk to her later and we hung up the phone. I thought long and hard about whether I was ready to go home.

And actually I didn't think long, I just thought hard. I looked at the square footage of my apartment closing in on me; I felt the squeeze of the city outside. I liked talking about my life to people, telling them about my urban adventures and how—ha, ha, ha—something as simple as buying milk could turn into a two-hour adventure. I liked the talk more than I actually liked finding myself trapped in the two-hour string of calamites that kept me from simply purchasing milk *like a normal person*.

I called her back five minutes later.

"I was wrong," I said. "I'm ready to move home and it's going to be nice to spend time in the South again."

"Well," she answered, "you're going to have to do something about how you talk before you get back down here. No one's going to understand you as long as you insist on properly pronouncing all your vowels. I'm not gonna want to take you out in public that way."

And so it was decided; I was trading in the fantasy for down-home reality.

I would buy a one-way ticket home and take up residence in my parents' guest bedroom. And I would keep my fingers crossed that my stay would be long enough to sort out what I wanted to be doing and where I wanted to be living, but short enough that the guest bedroom never started to feel like my own. I was homeward bound, a twenty-eight-year-old hobo seeking shelter under her parents' roof.

And where exactly in the United States was this roof? Well, the wheels on the bus go round and round, round and round, round and round. And sometimes those wheels go round and round in reverse.

A few months before I decided to move in with them, my parents had returned to a state I thought I'd said goodbye to the day I graduated from high school: Oklahoma.

When I got on the plane at LaGuardia I was officially trading tall buildings for cornfields. Sushi restaurants for barbeque joints. People who yelled at you on the street for a wind that blew through plains so hard and fast it actually howled.

I wouldn't be the only one with culture shock. My parents had most recently been living in Malaysia so they were suffering, um, I mean *working through,* an adjustment period as well.

From my window seat, I watched airline workers load the last of the suitcases and took a deep breath. My boxes had been shipped. Once the plane took off nothing of mine would be left on the island.

Almost like the storybook had been dropped in the Hudson, and the words in my fairy tale had never existed at all.

I saw my parents as soon as I entered the baggage claim at the Tulsa airport. They had driven the hour to pick me up, and after we ate dinner we would drive the hour back to the small town where they lived.

"Couldn't Dad's company have moved you guys to Miami? Maybe somewhere in California?" I asked after I hugged them.

"Well dear," my mother answered, "your father and I are looking on the bright side. If we lived somewhere like Miami or California, there's a good chance you'd decide to stay forever."

"Not that there's anything wrong with that," my dad interjected.

"Plus," my mom reminded me, "you said you were okay with the South."

"Lots of people don't consider Oklahoma to be Southern," I said. But I saw the look she flashed to my dad. It said, "Just because she's an adult doesn't mean we can't whip her into shape."

CALL ME A SQUATTER

"You're right, Mom," I said. "I did say I was okay with it, and I am."

We gathered my bags at the terminal while my mom held a one-sided debate with herself about where we should get dinner. From what I could tell, the options were Italian and Mexican, but both were chain restaurants and she worried they would be bland.

"Not that there's anything wrong with that," my dad responded to her monologue.

"Is that your phrase of the day?" I asked.

"More like a phrase of the month," he replied. "I'm working on being more accepting," he said.

"That's probably a good thing," I answered. A woman with a pink sweatshirt that matched her pink sneakers walked by and my eyes got as big as two fists, my eyebrows raised all the way to my bangs. Dear God, what had I done.

By the time we got to the car, my mom announced that we were going for bland Mexican over bland Italian because any one of us could make a bland bowl of spaghetti at home.

My dad opened his mouth to speak.

"Let me guess," I said. "There's nothing wrong with a bowl of bland spaghetti."

"No," he said. "I was just going to say that I'm driving. You haven't been behind the wheel in a couple years, and you weren't such a great driver in the first place."

I heaved one suitcase into the trunk and then the other. They got into the front seats and before I closed the trunk I turned to the right. East of the airport was nothing—just flat fields.

I was a long way from the tall buildings I'd grown accustomed to.

Not that there's anything wrong with that, I told myself.

I hoped it wouldn't take long for me to actually believe that.

We can't all be winners every day. I know that. The time I lost my cell phone in the back seat of a cab that sped away too fast I didn't throw myself on the sidewalk and start screaming the tune of the ringtone I'd never hear again. When I've lost weight during the week—the only time being a loser is a good thing—only to gain it right back over the weekend, I don't stand in front of my bathroom mirror in a bikini to torture myself.

But there was no stopping the mental anguish the morning I woke up in my parents' house and realized there was no return ticket to take me away. It was like a steamroller drove full speed ahead and crushed every hope I'd had for myself since departing for college.

I'd gone away from home, lived on my own, and established independence only to find myself back under their roof. Three steps forward. Four hundred steps back.

"I'm a loser," I announced to my mother. I had finally dragged myself out of bed, put the clothes from the night before that were on the floor back on my body and walked downstairs.

"That's harsh, honey," my mother said. "It isn't that you are a loser, you just aren't winning anything at the moment."

I considered her words. Then I realized it was just a gussied-up way of saying I was a loser.

"Maybe I should start small," I said. "You know, find something little that I can win at. I could take up a hobby."

Like blowing spit bubbles. Or playing *Dr. Mario* until all hours of the night. Whenever there's a movie about adults who still live with their parents it seems like video games are a main method of entertainment. Of course, those characters are usually played by someone like Matthew McConaughey, who would still manage to be cool even if his only worldly possession was a joystick.

I wondered what skills I had that I could turn into hobbies. My ability to fight the crowds for a seat on the subway was officially useless. Take me out of an urban environment and put me in, oh,

CALL ME A SQUATTER

I don't know—*Oklahoma*—and I wasn't sure what I had to offer. I didn't fish. I didn't hunt. I wasn't sure I supported camouflage as a design theme.

When I really thought about it, I wasn't even sure I could deliver on my promise of blowing a spit bubble. It had been at least two decades since I tried.

My mom waited a while before saying anything. "A hobby," she repeated.

"Are you paying attention Mom?" I asked. When I was in high school I'd come down in the morning and have her full attention. I hoped this wasn't indicative of disinterest that had formed in my absence. I could have stayed in Soho if I wanted to talk to myself.

"Of course I'm listening, dear. You want a hobby. I was just remembering the time your father said he wanted a hobby. That was when we decided to have children."

I was pretty sure that my being a hobby for my parents was less than one step away from being a loser.

"I don't think my hopes lie in procreation," I said. "In case you haven't noticed, there's not really a candidate for baby making in the picture right now."

It was more than just the lack of boyfriend. I hadn't even *said* the word "baby" in front of a male since I forced my brother to play house with me when we were kids. Any time it crossed my mind while living in New York, I'd do a double slap across my face and bite my tongue. If single men freaked out when someone floated the idea of a relationship, I figured saying you wanted a baby someday was like wearing a sign on your head that advertised SHE'S A LIVE ONE, AND WATCH OUT, SOUNDS LIKE SHE'S GOT LIVE EGGS, TOO. It was a guarantee that you'd go home alone, *maybe* with a kiss on the cheek, definitely not with plans for another date.

My mother gave me a look that asked me to please stop digging the knife in her heart and twisting, twisting, twisting.

"One day, Mom," I promised. "My hopes will lie in procreation one day. Just not today."

I decided that maybe running could be a new hobby for me. In Oklahoma there were miles of dirt roads I could pound away on. The treadmills in New York had bored me. One stick figure after another running, running, running, while they answered emails, read books, and probably figured out ways to set up nonprofit organizations that would save dying babies in Zimbabwe *all at the same time.* The intensity had intimidated me—sending me first to the treadmill in the corner of the gym and then out of the gym entirely. But surely running here on the city streets would be an entirely different experience, and so I floated the idea.

"You'd have to wake up early," she said. "By noon it's almost a hundred degrees outside."

"Knitting?" I asked. "It's an air-conditioned event."

"Are you going to say basket weaving next?"

"Actually, I was going to suggest cooking."

At that she just raised an eyebrow. "Did you even turn the stove on in your last apartment?"

I ignored the jab. There had been plenty of apartments where I turned on the stove too many times. Hadn't I almost burned down the building in Seattle? *So there.*

"You know, getting a job could always be your new hobby," she suggested.

"I plan on getting a job, but the idea is that I need a small victory, or maybe a series of small victories, to work my way up to the larger victory."

"Dating is an option," she suggested. "A date offers countless opportunities for small victories."

I'd dated in Oklahoma before. My memories were of guys who chewed tobacco and talked about how great they were at the high school sports they played. I imagined little had changed. We weren't in high school anymore, but I was willing to bet that their

CALL ME A SQUATTER

favorite topic of conversation was how great they had been back in the day. The day that was now long, long ago.

"It seems counterproductive to try and meet an Oklahoma man I would like, if the point is actually to leave Oklahoma."

My mom stood up from the table. "I've got it," she said. She walked to the counter and picked up a piece of paper. "I know a way we can guarantee at least fifty small victories today. You can purchase every item on the grocery list."

The steamroller had pulled all the way through my brain, and now it was flipping into reverse, just to make sure there were no missed spots.

She put the grocery list in front of me and left the room to get on with her own life. I didn't move, mainly because I didn't have much of a life to get on with.

Leaving the house would mean seeing people in the outside world. It would mean that people in the outside world could see me. There would be visual confirmation that I was living in Oklahoma. I started a list of things I'd thought I hated about New York, but now realized I missed.

If only I could be picked up by an angry Pakistani cab driver.

If only my blood pressure could double just from stepping out my front door.

If only a rat would run across the top of my flip-flops while I waited for the subway.

My mom popped her head back into the room. "The car keys are in my purse," she suggested with a smile.

And I gave her a fake smile back. "I was thinking about not leaving the house today," I said.

"Your second-best idea of the day—right up there with knitting. You really are on a roll." Then she shooed me from the room with her hand. I found the biggest sunglasses I owned to hide my face. Then I ventured outside.

JUST DON'T CALL ME MA'AM

My parents' town had one main road where commerce was centered. I drove down the road and passed a fast-food restaurant, a dollar store, another fast-food restaurant.

I mentally flipped through the shops on my street in Soho. A wine bar, a Tibetan shop, a coffeehouse that specialized in scones and pastries.

What did living in a world of dollar stores and fast-food restaurants say about my life? That I valued quantity over quality? That the most important selling point of a menu was that items could be grouped into combinations and super-sized for an extra forty-nine cents?

I started to panic. I chose not to remember that there had, in fact, been a time when I considered fast food a special occasion.

Long before I'd been trained to appreciate the world of difference between a tuna carpaccio and a tuna salad sandwich from Subway, I used to look forward to the afternoons when I got a Taco Bell burrito for an after-school snack. The only thing better than cartoons on a Saturday morning was waking up to an egg biscuit from McDonald's.

And in the summers when I was growing up and would spend weeks at Camp Grandma, these fast-food meals weren't as common as they were at home so they were even more precious. Her house was stocked with all the junk food a granddaughter could want, but I still missed the excitement of a restaurant. Choosing from all the selections! Eating a main course that's different from everyone else at the table! My grandmother didn't understand why you'd ever want a stranger to handle your food, but clearly I begged often enough because we'd wind up at the Dairy Queen in Kountze—the closest town to wear she lived—often enough.

Kountze was only twenty minutes away, but it usually took us forty minutes to get there. My grandmother is known for wisdom, not speed. And I am known for frequent bathroom breaks during road trips. Even road trips that only span twenty miles.

CALL ME A SQUATTER

The entire time her sedan inched along the highway, she would be asking me questions about the menu at Dairy Queen.

What was I going to eat?

What did I think she should order?

And one more time, why was any of this food better than what we could have eaten at home?

It exasperated me that Grandma didn't go to restaurants more often. If I lived in the woods and there was only one fast-food joint in the county, I'd know every item on the menu by heart and I probably would have tried each of 'em at least once.

But these trips were the only time I ever saw my grandma in a restaurant, much less eating fast food. It was like how she'd start sweating for no reason and blame it on something called a hot flash, and when she'd sit me down with an old picture album and take me through all the names of people on the pages over and over again so I'd be sure to remember. Some of the things Grandma did simply made no sense to me.

When we *finally* got within sight of the Dairy Queen sign I'd start to tap my foot and rock back and forth in the front seat. "We're almost there, we're almost there!" I'd squeal, with visions of parfaits dancing in my head.

There were lots of summer trips to Dairy Queen that blurred together in a haze of fried-food goodness, but there is one trip I can't forget. It was during the glory years of Camp Grandma when I was about seven or eight. That was when the week away was the perfect mix of freedom and independence of leaving my everyday home and yet I still had someone to tuck me in at night. On this trip we went just for dessert instead of lunch. And so I ordered two different ice-cream treats loaded with ground-up bits of my favorite candy bars. I told my grandma that I would eat one at the restaurant and then take the other home and put it in the freezer for another day. But I knew that she drove too slow for the ice cream to make it home without melting. My secret plan was to eat both treats back-to-back.

Even at that young, delicate age, I was already in training for my freshman fifteen.

My grandmother ordered one small cup of plain vanilla ice cream.

"Don't you want chocolate chips in it, or hot fudge on top?" I asked. Like I said, there are some things about my grandma I just never could understand.

She ignored me and spoke to the cashier, "Just the small bowl of vanilla."

After my grandma paid we sat down at a booth that gave me a clear view of the counter. That way I could see our food before they had time to say our number into the microphone. Once it was ready, I jumped up and retrieved the treats from the counter. Then I carefully picked out spoons and napkins, and carried the tray back to the table. It was the only time I ever got to serve my grandma any food.

Right after I started to eat, the door to the restaurant opened and the bell chimed. Not much out of the ordinary about that, except it wasn't a normal customer who walked in. This customer was someone that everyone in town knew, one of the drunks who hung out in the bars and slept in a trailer home. A face that had been around town for decades, but was never especially welcome.

Because I didn't actually live in town, I didn't know any of this. Not to mention that I would have been too young to understand anyway. All I knew was that when the man walked up to the counter he smelled bad. Real bad. And my nose did more than go on red alert, it wrinkled up in a loud, snobby statement of disgust. I leaned forward to my grandma, and after I had swallowed a bite of ice cream I said, in an extremely loud (and likely irritated) voice, "*Some*-body forgot to take a shower."

CALL ME A SQUATTER

Not an especially funny statement. Or insightful. Pretty much just stupid.

But I remember that I expected her to laugh. I really expected her to think I was funny for what I had said. Either at the man's expense, or at my boldness to actually say what everyone else in the restaurant was thinking.

I expected agreement, but I got the opposite. As soon as I saw her lips tighten into a straight line, I knew I'd done wrong.

Everyone in the restaurant had heard me. And in a town that small, making a rude comment that is overheard by five people is like shouting it to the whole population. When I spoke, the man had stopped walking and looked at the floor. Then he turned around and left the Dairy Queen.

My grandmother reached across the table and grabbed the wrist that was holding the spoon. She took the spoon out of my hand, put it back in the ice cream treat, and then took all of our food to the trashcan. When she came back to the table she did not sit down. She waited without speaking until I stood at her side and then followed her out of the restaurant to the car. As soon as I opened my door, the heat that had been bunching up inside the car hit my face. And that was about the same time the tears came. When we were settled inside with our seatbelts fastened, my grandma started the ignition, but before she put the car in gear she spoke to me.

"Why would you think you were better than somebody? Because you had a shower today? Because you have the money for two ice-cream treats instead of just one?"

She turned to look at me then. "No granddaughter of mine makes a joke out of another person. Do you understand me?"

I nodded my head yes.

"I want to hear you say that you understand me."

"I understand you, Grandma." The switch flipped, and my tears hit high gear.

It wasn't until we'd driven all the way home, and I'd almost peed in my pants because I had to go to the bathroom so bad but didn't dare to ask, that she reached in her purse and handed me a tissue. She said that she just wanted me to treat people right, the way I would want to be treated by them. And I knew she wasn't upset with me anymore by the time she tucked me into bed. But she did not take me back to Dairy Queen during that trip.

Through all the long years of junior high and high school, when mockery is practically a pastime for most, I remembered that lesson. When I would fall prey and engage, my penance would not be Hail Marys. Instead I'd think of the reproach on my grandma's face that day.

But soon enough I got all caught up in my life and in moving to big, fancy, faraway cities and before I knew it, that day at the Dairy Queen had been forgotten faster than a rattlesnake will cross a creek.

Back in Oklahoma, I completed the grocery store trip for my mother. And I bought every item on her list. And then the next day I went to Wal-Mart. The day after that I met my dad for lunch at the Pizza Hut. Days turned to weeks and those turned into a month. But instead of taking up new hobbies, I decided to stay rooted in old ways. Everywhere I went, I wrinkled my nose.

Cashiers who were inefficient when they counted out change too slow, or just completely incorrectly.

Country people who rode into town with their truck windows down and animals in the back.

The teenagers who sat in parking lots on Saturday nights, flirting with each other and waiting to see if someone could score a six-pack of beers.

It all reminded me of what I'd initially wanted to flee from, so I held on tighter to the person I'd become in the time I was away. I refused to wear casual clothes even when we were going to a bar for a beer. I'd put on a skirt and a pair of high heels. In Oklahoma, that kind of outfit is usually reserved for activities that happen in churches: sermons, deaths, and weddings.

When people offered me a friendly smile, I'd return it with a quick upturn of the mouth. I wore my iPod everywhere to try and keep people from making conversation. In New York City, an iPod in your ears was code for "Please do not bother me." In Oklahoma, people probably thought I was an idiot for wearing it in the aisles of Wal-Mart because how could I hear the special sale announcements over the intercom system? I spent my spare time trying to stay connected to the world I'd known, reading every magazine, blog, and newspaper I could find.

"A new restaurant opened up," I would tell my mother.

"Really?" she'd ask. "I hadn't heard a word about that."

"In the West Village. A few blocks from where I used to live. An Italian place that's getting really good reviews."

She would roll her eyes and leave the room.

My dad would mention that there was a band playing downtown, and I would remind him that it wasn't actually a band, more a group of people who all happen to know how to play instruments. Then I would go upstairs and load more indie music onto my iPod. I wasn't even sure if I liked the music, I just knew it was what *everyone* was listening to. Everyone not stuck in Oklahoma.

Then my phone rang. My best friend who still lived in New York was on the other end of the line. There was a party that weekend, did I want to take a break from Oklahoma and come to town?

Did pigs like to roll in shit?

Forget the fact that I'd only been gone a month. Forget the fact that I really shouldn't be spending my unemployment check on over-priced martinis in Manhattan. I got on the Internet and found the cheapest ticket that I could. Four days later I was back

JUST DON'T CALL ME MA'AM

in the city, and for, oh, about twenty minutes, it was like I had never left.

The hullabaloo.

The buildings.

The beginning of that story in my brain: Once upon a time, a girl who lived in a very small town packed up her bags and moved to New York City.

I took a cab to a bar in my best friend's neighborhood. When she was done with work, she would meet me there.

In the meantime, my plan was to strike up conversation with someone, anyone, who would immediately think "git" to be a charming piece of antiquated verbak kitsch and not an appropriate substitution for "get," "acquire," or "obtain."

There are cities in America where bars don't fill up until the sun goes down, luckily for me that day, New York is not one of those cities. As soon as I rolled my suitcase up to the bar and ordered a drink a man sitting two barstools down asked me whether I was coming or going.

"I just flew into town," I offered.

He was wearing a tight-fitting dress shirt, untucked with a pair of jeans and high-top Converse. No Wranglers. No white T-shirts splattered with paint. No work boots in sight.

I settled into my drink and smiled at him, wondering if this conversation could evolve into a flirtation.

"Where'd you fly from?" he asked.

I took a sip. "You don't want to know," I said.

He said he did want to know and I said that no, really, he didn't want to know. He insisted that he did, so I admitted I was flying in from Oklahoma.

He took a drink and then looked my way with a half smile. Probably asking himself if he actually wanted the answer to the question he was about to ask.

CALL ME A SQUATTER

"So," he said, "what could you possibly have been doing with yourself in Oklahoma?" he asked.

I considered my options. I could lie, and say that I had a work trip. I could say that my very important job needed me to be there for a very important meeting and that I flew in and out as quickly as possible.

Or I could tell the truth and admit I had moved in with my parents to deal with a mini career crisis and that this weekend was actually designed as a vacation from that crisis.

No need to guess which response would be an immediate end to any possible flirtation.

I looked at my suitcase, and at the outfit I'd picked out for the plane ride. It was carefully constructed so I wouldn't arrive in Manhattan looking like I'd been in Oklahoma just four hours before.

"Funny thing," I said. "I actually live in Oklahoma."

"You're kidding," he said.

But I was not.

He made a half-hearted attempt at a recovery. "Well, um, what do you do there?"

I took a big gulp of my drink and then put the glass back on the counter. "Funny thing about that, too. You see, I'm unemployed at the moment and live in my parents' house. So I do some errands and random chores. I spend a lot of time thinking about what I want to do with my life. Occasionally I consider taking up a hobby. Right now woodworking seems to be in the lead."

He looked to the other corner of the bar, started to examine the bottles behind the bar.

"You can make all kinds of stuff. Jewelry boxes. Um, boxes for keys and random stuff." I cleared my throat. "Um, did I mention jewelry boxes."

He continued to examine the bar when he spoke. "Cool," he said. "I get it, I mean, everybody's got to figure their shit out."

But he was only being polite. He finished his drink and left the bar with a wave, instead of a goodbye. My answer wasn't good enough for him, but it was the only answer I had to give. It was the truth. I was from Oklahoma, no matter how I tried to dress it up or what iPod soundtrack I set my day to. Wranglers. Work boots. Tobacco chew. Wal-Marts that were the best shopping in town. I'd signed up for all of it; maybe it was time for me to stop snubbing it.

I wondered what my grandma would say if she'd seen the way I'd been acting for the last month. She'd seen me graduate from high school in Oklahoma, so I guess she'd be nothing short of mortified. "Where you come from is who you are," she was fond of saying. "The rest of it's just fluff."

I'd been way too caught up in the fluff, and so I committed to starting to figure out the real questions once I got back to Oklahoma.

It didn't take my best friend much longer to arrive at the bar. She hugged me, ordered a drink, and immediately asked what I wanted to do for the weekend.

"I want to do everything," I said, "because I have a feeling I'm not going to be back for a while."

Since every one of the phone conversations my best friend and I had since I moved out of Manhattan revolved around the "what if" game—What if I moved back to New York, what neighborhood would I live in? What job would I work at? What restaurant would become my Sunday night favorite?—she was quick to question what happened to me since our last conversation.

"What's up?" she asked.

"Nothing's up," I answered. "It just took me being here for it to finally sink in that this isn't my home anymore."

I bought a postcard on my way back through LaGuardia. I paid more for it than a hamburger would cost me at any Dairy Queen. The postcard is jumbo-sized, and it has a view of downtown New

CALL ME A SQUATTER

York City on it. I don't keep it in plain view, but I see it most every day when I open a drawer where I keep makeup and jewelry; a friendly reminder that I don't have to dress like the person I was when I lived there to remember the lessons I picked up along the way.

The postcard is nowhere near the size of the mural that was on the wall of my bedroom when I lived in Louisiana, but it serves the same purpose. Except now when I see that view I know that being there won't fix my problems or make life perfect.

Unfortunately, or fortunately, that part of the equation was up to me. Which is exactly why as soon as I got back to my parents' house, I wallpapered a life-size mural of myself on the guest bedroom wall.

ADDENDUM: Some tips and tricks for adults on moving back in with your parents without losing your mind.

Granted, moving home with one's parents isn't something that many people will have to do in their lifetimes. The vast majority of the population are self-sufficient, independent adults who manage their finances and live in a way that protects their self-esteem from the crushing blow of retreating back under the same roof as their parents.

But for the rest of us, that small percentage of the world who hits a point in adulthood where they just don't want to be adults anymore and need a few days, weeks, or months off from life, I have a few suggestions for the sabbatical. For those who endure a year or more, I am truly in awe of your fortitude. My only advice to you is that you should be sure to remove all sharp objects from the drawers of your bedroom.

1) Look at errands as an escape, not a chore.

Don't say to yourself, "I can't believe I just put a six-pack of calcium milkshakes in the cart for my premenopausal mother." Instead, remind yourself that the grocery store can be a thirty-minute departure from staring at your computer screen and wondering why no one is emailing to tell you that they'd like to pay you a salary and also provide you health insurance.

2) Just because you are living at home, doesn't mean you'll be living on home-cooked meals.

This was totally shocking to me at first, because without thinking about it I had assumed that, at the very least, my mom would be pleased as punch to zap me a TV dinner, maybe share her TV tray with me, perhaps get me a second helping of microwave mashed potatoes when she got up for her own.

But apparently once my brother and I moved out of the house, she moved her pots and pans out as well.

One night, early in my stay, I got hungry around dinnertime so I went to the kitchen to see what was cooking. All I found was my father, shuffling around with some canned chili products in hand.

"Dad?" I asked. I imagine I had the same fear in my voice as the kids in those horror movies who wake up in the home alone to find a shadow in the kitchen. They know it's not Dad. They know it's a zombie there to kill them with an axe, or maybe a sledgehammer. But by saying "Dad" it's like holding on to one last straw of human hope that in the end everything might be A-okay.

My father turned around to look at me, "Yes?"

"What are you doing?" I wanted to know.

"Oh this?" He held up the canned chili. "I'm ready for dinner."

I asked if he wanted to cook something that was at least a mixture of products from different cans, instead of just one can dumped into a bowl.

"That would technically be cooking," he said. "And I prefer either microwaving the contents of one can or picking up Chinese food."

I guess he saw the disappointment on my face.

"I heard your mom made you eggs the other morning," he said, and I swear I saw wistful memories of days when the oven was used pass across his face. "You should feel really thankful for those eggs."

3) Your parents are your roommates, not your therapists.

My parents faked me out on this one. All those holidays I would come home and we'd chat, chat, chat into the night, and I'd tell them about my love problems or my life issues. Apparently, this was interesting for them when my visits were sporadic. On a daily basis, they were less than interested with up-to-the-minute reports on my mental health. Turns out, they had their own lives to live, and believe me, that concept took time for me to wrap my head around.

On top of that, when they did ask how I was feeling, they rarely commented like I wanted them to. I like it when people agree with me—not so much when they disagree. Possibly why I have never excelled at debate, conversation during an election year, or the endless communication with my Asian manicurist who also waxes my eyebrows. I'm helpless in my attempts to try to explain to this woman that I don't need to wax my upper lip because the hairs there are blonde. She does not agree. And she refuses to refer to it as my upper lip, *mustache* seems to works better for her.

My mother could only say so many times that life wasn't going to deliver a new job to the front door before I realized that I needed to find another shoulder to cry on. Preferably a shoulder of sympathy instead of tough love.

There are times in life you can handle the truth and there are times when avoidance of the truth is the key to sanity.

4a) Thinking about sex is like waving a steak in front of the face of a starving man, then telling him that the steak is actually soaked in a pesticide that could kill him.

If you believe what Hollywood tells you about living with your parents, then you probably believe that lots of adult children who live at home still find ways to have sex.

Granted, in the movies the dad is usually walking in on the characters in the act, or one of the ladies from the mother's Bunko party finds a used condom on the floor and hilarity ensues. There are "blunders" associated with sex, but the audience can rest assured that no one is being starved of sexual activity.

I went from feeling a tad bit hungry to being downright famished before I finally accepted there were no emergency UN food rations on the way. Not having sex was a repercussion of my living situation. Not as serious a repercussion as a constantly fluctuating sense of self-confidence, or being introduced to my parents' friends as the child "who almost got away." But still, serious.

4b) Vibrators are best left in the box.

And on the above note, never confuse a vibrator to be a viable solution for this sexless interim.

"Were you vacuuming upstairs?" my mom asks, a hint of this-is-to-good-to-be-true in her voice. Which, of course, it is.

"Um, no."

"Were you blow-drying your hair?"

"No. And I thought you were going to get your hair cut."

"The salon called and canceled the appointment, I guess the stylist was sick."

A long silence from me. "Oh," I finally say.

My mother contemplates whether to pursue the conversation. Her curiosity wins the battle against protecting my privacy. "So, was that noise coming from a sewing machine?"

5) Your sanity? Priceless.

Obviously, living with your parents saves money on rent. But if you are looking to save money on other expenses, moving in with your family isn't necessarily a money-saving decision.

It's kind of like figuring out rent in New York City. The actual dollar figure you estimate for rent expenses should also include money for the things you do to escape the small size of your apartment. Like when the walls are closing in and you pay a ridiculous amount of money to sit in a wine bar with open windows. Or when you realize you are sitting in a puddle of sweat because the sun is shining on every square inch of your apartment and the super won't fix the air-conditioning, so you go to the movies.

Rent + Cost of wine + Movie tickets = Actual rent.

And that's how it is when you live with your parents. You feel like you are living on the cheap until you realize that if you are going to eat anything besides canned green beans you have to buy that food yourself. And then every time you get the feeling that your mom is about to mention something about doing laundry or making yourself useful you go screaming out of the house searching for distraction. All those eyebrow waxes and trips to Wal-Mart? Trust me, they can add up.

Chapter 8

Call Me a Sword-Sharpener

Some of my friends are short. Some are tall. I have friends who are Jewish, Catholic, Muslim, and Baptist—though they tend to enjoy my humor more if they are lapsed Baptists. There are brunettes and blondes, some with jet-black hair that fades to a peroxide blonde—a look I wish I was cutting edge enough to pull off—and a couple with God-given gorgeous black locks and a few redheads to boot (mostly so I can live in constant envy of their perfectly freckled complexions). Analytical minds, creative minds, dirty minds, and a handful of people who—on occasion—drink themselves out of their minds. Living all over the country they've introduced me to a wide smattering of opinions, beliefs, and points of view. Do you keep a gun in your car? If you're a college friend from Texas, probably yes. If you're a female coworker I met in New York, it's not far-fetched that you've never even seen a gun except on the movie screen.

I enjoy having friends who offer different perspectives on topics ranging from the merits of fantasy sports leagues to the tendency of Southern women to procreate at surprisingly young ages. These perspectives can change faster than a pat of butter'll sizzle in the pan, and usually that's fine by me. There is only one topic that I do not leave to chance. I know for certain which side of the online dating fence every one of my friends chooses to stand on.

In the beginning, I was naive to the public perception of online dating. I thought people in my life would treat it like any other new fad I tried on for size. If friends would listen to my obsessive ramblings on the hair removal lotion I bought from a late-night infomercial, then surely they'd care to hear more about my experiences in online dating.

I quickly discovered this was not the case.

There were those who were open to it and those who were not. Those who were open to meeting people online were those friends who were single and also trying online dating for the first, fifth, or five hundredth time. These were the friends with whom I could joke around about it. Ha-ha, kind of funny that we now shop online for more than just shoes and purses. Ha. Shopping for men, no sales tax included! Ha. Ha. Big gulp of martini. Ha.

But then there was the sect of my friends that didn't understand online dating no matter how many ways I tried to slice it. I'd explain that it was simply a new way to meet people, and I'd get a blank stare. I billed it as a more efficient dating method: meeting someone online meant I could figure out if I had things in common with a person before I wasted a Saturday night discussing the pros and cons of a euro-based economy when the only real-world ramification that interested me was how far my dollar

JUST DON'T CALL ME MA'AM

would stretch for a pint of Guinness at a London pub. Still nothing but blank stares.

This group of friends is composed of the people who were blessed with simple, relatively low-stress dating lives. They met their significant others in high school, college, or in the first years after college. Most of the people I know who fall in this category are Southern. They sympathize with the plight of the modern dater, but usually tack an "I have no idea what I would do if I ever had to be single again" onto those sympathies, so there is no confusion to the fact that they would rather sit naked in an ice bath for all eternity than make small talk with a stranger who has equal chance of either not being seen again after the night is over, or being naked in their beds by the stroke of midnight.

I do see where this group of friends is coming from. Dating isn't necessarily a "good time" like, say, going waterskiing, or "entertaining" like playing Pin The Tail On The Paparazzi Shot with pictures of Paris Hilton and a bottle of Beam. But if you are a single person who would like companionship for a Saturday night, not to mention the rest of your life, then dating is something that must be endured. The other option is to mail-order a spouse from Eastern Europe—and to the souls who embark on that adventure I wish you good luck and a mighty thorough dictionary for the language of your betrothed.

For a long time I stood tall with the friends who believed the right man would waltz into our lives at the right time. No extra effort required. But then I watched enough Saturday nights pass me by to realize that if I didn't jump on the train it would be me and my shriveling ovaries 'til death did us part. Amen.

The online world had seemed like a natural fit for me. Instead of picking up the phone to say hello to friends, I had grown accustomed to simply sending emails. I shopped online. I read the newspaper online. I even took a few online classes to save the hassle of moving my body from the couch to a classroom. In all

CALL ME A SWORD-SHARPENER

these ways I gladly eschewed the threat of carpal tunnel so I could type my way to connections with the outside world. But when it came to the love connection, I held out on the belief that I could meet a man the old-fashioned way: by getting really drunk and stumbling into Mr. Right on my way to the bathroom.

Plan B was for a hot guy to show up at my grocery store, or maybe appear at the dryer next to mine at the Laundromat. It happened that way for people in television commercials, there was every reason to believe love could magically materialize for me. Maybe that was the reason I'd left New York for a sabbatical in Oklahoma and then moved on to try out a new job in Denver. A Colorado man! Of course! Who also liked unscented detergent and would share his dryer sheets with me when I left mine at home!

And if someone asked me to explain this discrepancy in my life—why I was comfortable searching for satisfaction online in every arena except romance—I wouldn't point the finger at myself, oh no, I would steer toward the story of how the people who brought me into this world were brought to each other.

If my mother and my father had signed up for an online dating site that matched people based on personality characteristics, life goals, and hobbies, they never would have been paired together. Not even the smartest software could have guessed they'd still be waking up in the same bed after thirty-five years, because the only things they had in common when they met were that both of them inhaled oxygen and exhaled carbon dioxide, and each had chosen to go to college in a small Louisiana town. When they met, my mom was quiet with an interest in the sciences. My father's main interest was in driving fast cars and chasing busty blonde women all over town. Did I mention that my mother is a brunette?

They met on a summer night when people gathered at the local bar because it was the only place serving relief from the humidity that moved in from the marshes. My mother normally would not

JUST DON'T CALL ME MA'AM

have followed this crowd, but she was on a date with a man from one of her classes, and he suggested they go there for a drink. As my father tells the story, he spotted my mother from his seat at the bar. He contends he was nursing a beer after a long day of work to earn money for his tuition. Of course, my mother claims he was more than a few beers into an all-night party with the loudest group of hell-raisers in town.

This is the point in the telling of the story when my mother usually crosses her arms and waits for my father to acquiesce to her version of events. In the old days, my father would have stubbornly stood his ground, insisting that his memories of being an upstanding, considerate citizen were correct. He has since matured into a wiser, more sane man, and is now content to see the error in that way. He and his friends were loud. They were hell-raisers.

When my mother's date went to the restroom my father seized the opportunity to approach her. He asked if he could sit down and my mother declared the seat at her table already taken; she suggested that my father look elsewhere for entertainment. Being a man with an ego to protect he disappeared into the crowd, but not for long. About thirty minutes later my father emerged from the throngs of college drinkers with one woman under each arm, all three of them heading out to the parking lot. As their group passed my mother and her date, my dad looked her in the eyes and said, "This is what you're missing out on, chickadee."

It's difficult to know which part of this exchange melted my mother's heart. Perhaps the use of such a respectful term, or maybe it was the classiness and high moral fortitude my father displayed by escorting not one, but two, other women home for the night. But my mother was caught. And that hook's stayed in her for the last thirty-five years.

Put that scenario online and they never would have made it past the initial profile perusal. My father would've had a handle like "chickadeesloveme123" and my mom would have claimed to

CALL ME A SWORD-SHARPENER

be more interested in finding study buddies than true love. There would be no faster death for an online dating relationship than to leave the bar with a different person—the technological equivalent of not reading hundreds of emails from virtual suitors because you are involved in an email correspondence with the first man who responded to your profile.

With that in mind, I stood strong against online dating. When my friends went looking for love online, I visited more coffee shops and hung out in the park, trying to look approachable. They started getting dates. I got over-caffeinated and sunburned from sitting too long in the sun. And on Sunday mornings I would call my mother from my new home in Colorado to complain that the only thing I had to snuggle up with the night before was a container of pad thai.

One Sunday she finally had enough, "You can't wait for friends and men to find you," she said. "*You* need to find *them*."

I explained I had tried to converse with the Thai deliveryman and instead of matching my commentary on the weather, he'd just dropped an extra fortune cookie in my bag and pedaled away.

"There is a whole world of people online, and surely one of them would be a man nice enough to go on a first date with."

"But online dating is where all the lonely people go," I argued.

"Silly me," my mother said. "All this time I thought lonely people were waiting at their front doors with the expectation that their Thai deliveryman might turn into a friend."

I knew my mother was right. But even though all my friends were online looking for people to connect with, and I knew love had been found online by plenty of normal people—people who went to jobs, paid bills, and bought bananas at the grocery store—my reservations were as stubborn as a cow's. No amount of pushing was going to tip me to the other side.

I wanted love to find me.

I wanted love to seek me out in a bar and then when I turned it down I wanted it to throw a tantrum in the form of two busty, blonde women.

I wanted the love that my parents had, which was one of the only loves I'd ever seen that actually worked out. Maybe for the sheer fact that it wasn't supposed to work out at all.

My mother didn't want arguments. "You'll never know what's out there unless you try it," she said.

"Let's say," I started, "let's just say that you and Dad got divorced tomorrow."

I waited for her to dispute the possibility of this fact, but she remained silent. Chances were good he hadn't bothered to unload the dishwasher in a while.

"If you and Dad were divorced tomorrow, would you go online and date?" I asked.

She remained silent for a second. I contemplated that something more serious than an overcrowded dishwasher had occurred, perhaps he had forgotten an anniversary or didn't notice her most recent haircut.

But then she spoke, "If your father and I were divorced tomorrow, I'd get on a plane and fly to a beach far, far away for a month. Then I'd come back home and spread my clothes out in every drawer and closet in this house because all the space would be mine. And then every night for a year I would go to sleep in the middle of the bed because no one would be there to hog the space," she paused for a moment. "And then after that year was up, I would probably call your father and ask him to come home."

"So you wouldn't date online. Even for conversation, or just a friendly face in the year before you begged for him back."

"That's right," she said, "I would just enjoy my peace and quiet. I would make the most of the time while I was preparing to grovel."

"But you're telling me to go online, even though it's nothing you would consider for yourself, even in your lowest, most groveling times."

"You and I are living different lives," she said. "Which is fortunate for two reasons."

"Yes?" I asked her to continue.

"When I was your age, I already had a three-year-old to keep track of. And dearest, I love you, but you have difficulty keeping track of your sunglasses."

True.

"And I got used to technology a lot later than you did. It took me long enough to figure out how to buy an airline ticket online, I can't imagine my learning curve for picking out a human being."

Slight confusion on the distinction between online dating and purchasing a man online, which would likely be a felony and probably not have the money-back guarantee I insist upon when shopping on the Internet. But still true.

My mother was right. If I was going to look for love in the modern world, I had to modernize my ideas about where I looked for romance. After a thorough application of antiaging moisturizer and a pep talk to my bathroom mirror, I took her advice and found a dating website where I could start my online dating career.

At first I thought building a profile for myself was going to be a rather demoralizing exercise. Kind of like a really dark night when you've had too much wine and so you start overanalyzing every part of your life that you wish to improve. Tomorrow. When your head isn't spinning. You can only do so much deconstruction of elusive intangibles like "happiness" or "man that has the potential to make me happy forever and ever and ever, amen" before the last drops of whimsy are squeezed out of your heart, and you're left with a pulsing cynicism in your chest.

Making my profile was nothing like that. A couple minutes into the process and I was as happy as a pig in shit. If you've never completed a dating profile online, I recommend you stop what you are doing right now, go to a computer, and immediately begin to enter in your information. Your husband, wife, boyfriend, girl-friend, or partner won't care as soon as they see the boost it gives your confidence. We're not talking about a couple rungs on the ladder, this is more like a shimmy up a sycamore.

I've been to therapy.

I've gone on spiritual quests to other countries searching for answers in temples, cathedrals, mosques, and overly-air conditioned shopping malls that sell American brand-name jeans for more than one of my paychecks.

But never before have I felt such absolution from any faults or flaws in my personality as when I began to put together my dating profile online. You have to pay for the experience, but hell, I've spent more money on a facial than I paid for this dating service. And when you're filling out an online profile you don't have to deal with the pain of anyone squeezing a blackhead; no one is going to suggest that you have damaged your skin beyond repair with overexposure to the sun. How would they even know you have sunspots? It's not like you have to put your actual picture with the profile. Maybe I *do* happen to bear a striking resemblance to Scarlett Johansson, thanks for noticing.

The dating website will start out slow, asking for information that's easy to share. You're giving your address, your credit card number. These are the easy things—the information we're used to typing in for everything from energy bills to energy supplements and energy-efficient vibrators, which will be delivered in three to five business days to your home in an unmarked (recyclable) box.

CALL ME A SWORD-SHARPENER

Once you're warmed up with the simple stuff, you start to move into the bigger questions. What are your hobbies? What is your profession? How much money do you make?

And this is where it got really uplifting for me. Up to that point my hobbies had included a lot of microwaving frozen meals, being a hermit with whatever book I was reading at the moment, some short jogs to learn the new neighborhood. I thought a lot about more aspirational hobbies, maybe learning to play chess or speak French. I had every intention that one day those activities would be a part of my day-to-day life. It just so happened that at that moment in time, the intention had not become reality.

But did the Internet need to know that teeny, tiny distinction?

After a couple minutes of crafting the perfect paragraph, I was back to being the woman I woke up as every January 1: athletic, witty, engaging, and making a salary close to the one I was fairly certain I'd earn by 2015. I decided to upload an actual picture of myself, but one that showed my best side—me on a beach vacation with a margarita in hand. Basically a 180 from how I look when I wake up in the morning, or after an especially long day at the office. And definitely not anywhere close to the look I give if someone wants to chat when I am running out the door with a million things on my to-do list and no caffeine in my veins.

Did I smoke cigarettes? There wasn't an option for "Occasionally when I am having a glass of wine," so I rounded down to "No."

Did I want to have kids? Of course, I wanted kids—forget the fact that every time I walked into a restaurant and saw a screaming toddler I ran out screaming myself. I had been thinking about the lifespan of my ovaries lately, that had to count for something.

I worked my way down the list and built the person I knew I had the potential to be, the woman that someday would stare back at me in the bathroom mirror.

And then the questions on the site shifted from myself to the person I hoped to meet on the site.

Ambitious? Check.

Funny? Check.

Athletic? Check.

Successful? Love it when the man can pick up his half of the check.

I momentarily forgot that every man I knew was actually a mix of these characteristics—occasionally a big serving of ambition arrived with a side order of slightly balding. And that funny to one person was not funny to the other—I prefer sarcasm and don't believe that a smiling emoticon makes any online message funnier; it actually has the opposite effect for me.

The description of my dream man ended up remarkably similar to how I always imagined George Clooney to be. Good looking, with a smile that hid a secret I would spend the rest of my life trying to figure out. Mystery, mixed with sexy, a touch of maturity, and a heck of a lot of interest in wooing me on the Italian Riviera.

In the real world, George Clooney would be so out of my ballpark it would be like trying to hit a homerun that stretched from Fenway to Boston Harbor. But this wasn't the real world anymore, this was the online dating world. And the George Clooney clone waiting on the other end of the Internet wasn't a long shot for the version of me that was a few pounds lighter, a couple IQ points smarter, and had a pair of breasts not yet pressed by the thumb of gravity.

Drawing this picture of myself launched me into a state of euphoria. I hadn't realized how great I could be, and all that I had to offer. *Of course,* the perfect man was out there waiting for the perfect me. Together we were going to conquer all the perfect-couple activities that came our way: ordering for each other in

CALL ME A SWORD-SHARPENER

restaurants, riding tandem bikes, taking Saturday trips to chain stores that sell home-improvement paraphernalia.

Online dating was the best thing that happened to my confidence since I got rid of the scale in my bathroom.

As I was patting myself on the back for being such a great person, an instant message came through from a friend. She wanted to know what I was doing.

I assumed that this friend was asking this question for the most obvious reasons: because she was a good friend who was actually interested in what I was doing with my Sunday night. This friend had been married for quite a long time, and usually enjoyed a belly laugh at the expense of whatever firecracker had most recently sizzled out in my dating universe. Colorado hadn't given me a lot of talking points yet, but this online dating thing had potential.

"Just took the plunge into online dating," I typed back.

While I waited for her response I pressed "Send" on my information, and all my hopes and desires for a relationship floated into the virtual universe.

After a minute of silence from my friend I went looking for her, "You there?" I typed.

"I never thought you would do online dating," she replied.

"Mom talked me into it. Trying something new, etc, etc."

"Is it safe?" she asked.

"Of course it's safe," I said.

For an instant I wondered if it was too late to get my information back, maybe sleep on it for a night.

"What kind of guys are you going to meet?" she asked.

"I was thinking George Clooney, but I'd be okay downgrading to more of a Casey Affleck, too."

"Ha," my friend wrote. "No chance. Did you think about joining a book club? Dating online just seems kind of . . . weird . . . "

JUST DON'T CALL ME MA'AM

I began to explain that things had changed since she was dating. For starters, guys had to pick us up at our apartments now, instead of the dormitories. And divorce rates have proven face-to-face chemistry to be faulty—at best. Book clubs were a great way to meet female friends, but the last guy I'd seen at a book club meeting was only there to prove to his boyfriend that he was the more avid Jane Austen fan of the two. But before I could start building my case, my friend logged off, typing that she and her hubby were going to have movie night.

Yeah. Have fun with that *body to keep you warm.*

Slowly my confidence drained out of my puffed-up chest and I returned to the reality of my B (but in the days before my period a C!)-cup.

Had my chronic state of singleton skewed my perspective on reality?

Was online dating actually a tattoo of desperation?

If it was a tattoo, could I possibly have it applied in disappearing ink?

Before my questions could stack into a pile of panic, I decided to call a friend who was an expert in online dating. She'd put her first profile online around the time Britney was still in pigtails and Catholic-school-girl skirts. While time had given Britney nothing but a befuddling choice for a (now ex-) husband, children, and headaches, my friend had emerged with a Wikipedia of online dating information.

When my friend answered, I practically jumped through the phone and shook her shoulders with the urgency of my question.

"Is it socially awkward to tell people that you are an online dater?" I asked.

"It depends on whether or not you're the kind of person who likes to start a conversation without saying hello."

"Hello," I said.

CALL ME A SWORD-SHARPENER

"Hi there," she answered. "And yes, it can be socially awkward depending on who you are talking to."

I told her that I'd just told a friend I was dating online and she'd acted like I'd announced a rather nasty case of the clap.

"Age?" she wanted to know.

"Of me or my friend?"

"Your friend. But you do realize you sound about seventy-two years old when you say 'the clap.'"

"Anyway," I interrupted. "My friend is twenty-nine."

"Married?"

"Yes," I said. "For eight years."

"Holy shit she's been married since she was twenty-one?"

Like I said, I have a group of friends with wide-ranging belief systems. This friend is liberal, lives in Seattle, and believes that you should know yourself before you can even start to know who you should marry. She does not believe people know themselves at twenty-one. But she's used to hearing things like this from my life as a Southern girl, so she got over the shock fairly quickly.

"You have to be careful telling certain groups of people that you are dating online," my friend started. "Anyone who was married before the age of twenty-five, people who haven't lived in big cities where it's hard to meet people—chances are good they were never desperate daters."

"Are we desperate daters?" I asked, wincing slightly.

"No," she said, "but people in those groups will think you are."

She advised me not to believe the hype. The dating ritual danced to a different beat these days. Online dating was so efficient that dating any other way was a waste of time and energy.

"Essentially you're saying that online dating is like TiVo for your vagina," I offered.

"Precisely," she said.

After we hung up I sat back and thought about online dating in this new light. I wondered if I wanted to engage in an activity that required me to act as though I had a dirty little secret that needed to be kept from the more traditional people in my life.

I'd been down that road before, when I kept a pretty big piece of my past hidden from the people in my life. The friends I'd met while living in Boston and New York, the other savvy singletons who spent time following design trends instead of baby jogger styles, these were the people who would cringe at the piece of my past I'd left in Texas when I graduated college—the four years I spent as a sorority girl.

When you are eighteen years old and enrolling in a college of thirty thousand people, of whom you know two, it makes a lot of sense to join a sorority. Once you get out of a sorority and into the real world, it makes a lot of sense to keep your sorority membership to yourself.

Moving out of Texas to a place where people don't think to ask you if you were in a sorority with any more frequency than they inquire about your last bowel movement allowed me to stow my sorority years along with my drawl and the fact that even though I'm a vegetarian now, I've done more than seen cooked snake, I've also nibbled on a bit and actually kind of liked it.

I was stealth in my practice of keeping my sorority secret. People asked about my college experience and I would tell long, elaborate stories about enduring the heat at football games. By the time I was done they'd usually meandered off, either mentally or physically, so there would be no follow-up danger. I threw away all my sorority T-shirts, and mentally erased the term "sorority sister" as a descriptor for certain college friends. They were classmates, or girls I bumped into on campus occasionally, never someone who lived by me in "the house" or was a "rush captain" for my chapter.

CALL ME A SWORD-SHARPENER

It wasn't that my entire sorority experience was awful. There were plenty of good moments—like the moment I walked out of the house for the last time, and the moment when I finally realized I could skip all the meetings I wanted and that they really only cared about collecting my dues.

But in Boston I already felt I was climbing an uphill battle as a Southern girl living up north with a funny way of speaking her words real-slowlike and an obsession with ranch salad dressing, which, apparently is like the antichrist of condiments. Ask for it in a traditional pizza parlor in Boston and you'll be lucky if they don't beat you with a frying pan on your way out the door. I had enough to overcome so I stayed mum on the sorority.

There was only one time when I let down my guard and the truth came out. It was seven years after I'd moved out of the South, and I was in Los Angeles on a business trip. Ten of us were having dinner at a sushi restaurant, all trying to drink enough on the expense account to feel vindicated for the loss of our free time.

One of the women at the table was new to the company and was playing the "Where are you from?" game with the woman seated across from her.

I usually try to avoid this game at all costs. Mostly because I moved around so much as a young person and I don't have one good answer to the "Where are you from?" question. I usually just pick one place I lived and go with it. Most often this place is Texas. And most often people's response to that answer is to ask something along the lines of, "Oh I know so-and-so from Texas. Do you know him/her/it/my great-aunt Edna?" Which, of course I don't, on account of there being close to *a bajillion people who live in Texas.*

The new hire mentioned that she'd gone to college in Oklahoma at the very moment I'd consumed enough vodka to forget that I don't participate in the "Where are you from?" game unless there is a very good-looking member of the male species on the other end, so I leaned forward and said, "Oh I went to high school in Oklahoma, what a funny coincidence."

Of course, our shared geography was neither funny nor coincidental. It could only be considered funny in the context of my other two options for discussion—the sleeping patterns of my boss's newborn baby or the work project we were all in Los Angeles to execute. And it was only coincidence if you managed to forget that there are fifty-two states in America and so statistically, eventually, you will bump into a person who spent their formative years surrounded by the same cow patties, wheat fields, or mountain ranges that were indigenous to your own upbringing.

She asked if I went to college in Oklahoma and I told her no, that after high school I'd gone to college at the University of Texas.

I'd been living outside the conversational reach of Southerners for so long, I'd forgotten the next, inevitable question. Thinking the exchange was over, I reached my chopsticks for some sushi.

"Were you in a sorority?" she asked, as I was picking up the sushi.

Suddenly I wished I could switch my place in the universe with the piece of the dead tuna in front of me. I was about to start frantically flip-flopping like a fish out of her home water.

My boss halted her description of the miracle mobile that was the trick for her baby to fall asleep, and turned her head in my direction.

Discussion on the shortcomings of our current clients came to a pause. This silence is an indication of the level of surprise at the table—getting advertising people to stop bitching about their clients is like finding the perfect apartment in the West Village on your first day of looking. And then finding out that the owner wants to give away the fancy furniture inside for free.

Everyone was waiting to see if I had an answer.

Surely not, they thought. Have we developed work friendships with a girl who ran around the South chanting songs and playing at a popularity contest well into her twenties? The doubt I felt in my belly was reflected in their eyes.

My years in the sorority house were like a Christmas tree that stays decorated year-round but gets tucked away in a closet throughout the eleven months of nonuse. I would roll it out when I visited with friends from Texas who had their own sordid sorority pasts, maybe turn on the lights if I was with family—the people who were forced by blood to accept me even if I had submerged the more unique parts of my personality in exchange for a secret sorority name and handshake. Otherwise, those experiences were supposed to stay hidden somewhere dark and quiet, only attracting attention from dust bunnies.

But this girl had already admitted to the fact that she was in a sorority, and for some reason, for some god-awful reason that suddenly welled in my chest, I couldn't leave her dangling out there all alone on the limb of this tree we'd both willingly climbed.

And after all, I liked my coworkers a lot. I wondered if maybe, somehow, I had misjudged the importance of keeping my sorority a secret. Perhaps if I let it out into the open then it would become one big, funny joke.

I swallowed the piece of fish and put my secret on the table.

"I was in a sorority," I said, and I exhaled the deep breath of denial that had been hiding inside for seven years. "Surprise?"

Then my boss took a sip of her drink, raised a chopstick in the air, and with a look that said she had always been proud of hiring me onto her team until that very moment, said, "You have got to be fucking kidding me." But she didn't say it all in one sentence. Each word was drawn out like a tight twist of the ole sorority handshake gone very wrong.

Unfortunately for me, I was not fucking kidding anyone. And so for the next two weeks, no one talked to me about work or the weather. People only wanted to know more about my former life as a sorority girl.

Were there pillow fights?

Girl-on-girl action?

Had anyone circled the cellulite on my legs as an initiation tactic?

People walked by my office and high-fived me while they yelled Greek letters at random. Alpha. Kappa. Sigma. Theta.

Isa Thisa Overa Yeta?

It wasn't until an illicit office romance was uncovered that the attention finally shifted from my past life to someone else's present woes. And I went back to being the slightly cynical, not gossip-worthy officemate I'd previously been.

There was not enough time in the world to explain to people that not every sorority girl is as superficial as MTV has stereotyped her to be. Just like there would not be time to convince people who didn't understand online dating that it was more than a bunch of lonely souls looking to meet up for coffee.

The only person worth convincing on both those counts was myself. Just like I'd learned to love the extra two inches on my hips as much as I appreciated the blue eyes passed down from my mother, I had to love my own unique combination of retired sorority girl who turned into a city girl, then a hippie, and a hipster, before finally settling on herself—a self that looks for dates in a variety of locations—offline, as well as online and in line at Target.

It was time for me to stop tiptoeing around people in my life, hiding the parts of myself that wouldn't be best received. For the first time in my life, I decided to live with a complete exposure clause.

The first step was to edit my online profile so that it was the most accurate representation possible. I took down the shot featuring the perfect hair day, perfect tan, perfect smile, and perfect outfit, and went for one that reflected how I looked when I walked

CALL ME A SWORD-SHARPENER

out of my house every morning. If a guy wasn't going to respond to that picture, then I wasn't going to like his response when I finally met him in person.

Unfortunately for my biceps, I was never going to be a mountaineering machine, and even if I upped my jogging by a few MPHs I'd still be a far cry from a serious runner. I listed more of my actual hobbies, like talking on the phone, pretending not to read tabloids, and getting pedicures.

A couple men emailed to say hi, and I emailed back. It was surprisingly similar to dating in the real world. Like walking on stilts in the beginning, with formal questions and canned jokes, but eventually the dialogue settled into a comfortable stroll. One conversation went so well we decided to meet in person so we could see if anything else clicked.

I mentioned over email that this was my first time as an online dater, so to excuse any awkwardness at the outset.

"Every girl says she's new to online dating," he said. "It's okay, you can admit the truth. I'm on this site, too, there's nothing to be embarrassed about."

"No really," I insisted, "this is all new to me. I have a new 'put it all out on the table' policy, so I would tell you if I were actually an old pro."

He seemed reassured that he didn't meet me during the more secretive phase in my life. Though, admittedly, that reply came a little slower than the others. Perhaps admitting you've previously tailored the truth depending on your audience wasn't the easiest pill for a prospective suitor to swallow.

We set up a date where we'd meet for drinks. I tried to look casual, but cute, and I read the newspaper that morning so I would have plenty of intelligent filler. To my surprise, when I arrived at the bar he had a water bottle with a beverage he'd brought from home.

"Go ahead and get a drink," he said.

"You aren't going to order anything?" I asked. I had assumed since he suggested a bar he had an intention of buying some kind of beverage (with or without alcohol). It would be reasonable for the establishment to have a policy where no shirt, no shoes, and/or no purchase equaled no entrance.

And that was the moment I realized why human beings occasionally tailor the truth for their audience—it is for our sanity as well as the sanity of those we speak to.

"I'm on the fourth day of a colon cleanse," he said. "But I didn't want to wait until my whole system was flushed to meet you. Considering what's been coming out of my body, that could be another couple weeks." And then he laughed, a surly slow cackle that I never would have attached to the meek manner in his online correspondence.

The bartender had walked over to take my order right as my date started to speak and heard the entire exchange. She gave me a look that said, "Get the hell out, and do it hella fast."

"I'll have a water," I said to her. And then I turned to my date. I did some mental calculations on how quickly I could get home to my pajamas, my book, and a microwave pizza.

"I didn't get a chance to mention in our emails," I said, "how much I loved being in a sorority in college. Want to hear some stories?"

As sure as the day is long, blatant honesty about the good, the bad, and the ugly in each of us is a double-edged sword we can wield as we see fit.

Chapter 9

Call Me the Birthday Girl

My first job out of college was as a junior copywriter, which meant that on the totem pole of people who created ads for our clients, I was on the very bottom rung. When the big boss brought his dog into the office for the day, it got more attention than I usually received.

Some days I got to do the copywriting part of my job, and then I'd type my little heart out, writing words that I hoped would sell products and eventually get me promoted to a high enough pay grade that I wouldn't have to choose between dinner or happy hour.

Other days I functioned more as the junior of the office, and on those days I would be sent into the bowels of Boston to buy an obscure T-shirt, or maybe a poster that someone was pretty sure he had seen a couple months ago at a certain store, but absolutely needed me to go locate right now so that an older creative team could explain their "brilliant" idea to our creative director. (The crucial element to a promotion in an advertising agency is always being able to spot a brilliant idea. Rule of thumb: Every idea presented by a more senior person is always brilliant, even when it's stupid.) On the days of errands I often wondered why I had bothered with the hassle of a degree. I could have survived just knowing how to hail a cab and being able to reach far enough behind my shoulder to attach a KICK ME sign to my own back.

At the agency I worked with account executives, designers, some finance guys, creative directors, and one president of the entire operation. In addition to these positions of necessity, which you could find at any agency in the country, this agency also staffed the one position that no group of people who aspire to call themselves an advertising agency can go without: a RAWLF (Receptionist All Would Like to Fuck). Make no mistake, this RAWLF is a far cry from the Ralph most typically found in cubicles across America. This is not a half-balding, pudgy fellow who wears Hawaiian shirts on Fridays, heats up a can of soup for lunch, and snorts when he laughs. The RAWLF of an advertising agency is a siren, the female who no man in the building can resist. When she eats soup, it's because some man has walked through five miles of snow and sleet to fetch it for her. When she wears Hawaiian-themed anything, it's because she's dressed up for an office theme party.

There are non-negotiable checkpoints on the road to becoming a RAWLF. Unless one has had excessive plastic surgery, a RAWLF must be under twenty-seven years of age. Her thighs should not touch when she walks, only when she sits with her legs provocatively crossed. And the RAWLF pout must be effortless, for the pout is the tool of intimidation that keeps all RAWLF fantasies alive, tempting males to believe that when they are asking her to reserve some airline travel, or order a catered breakfast for the client, the RAWLF is so disappointed to be talking to him instead of fucking him that her pout is the only way she can express the frustration of her loins.

I spent the first few months in awe of the RAWLF at my first agency. There I was, a Southern girl in a brand new part of the country. My thighs carried every piece of red velvet cake I'd ever eaten, and my pout was neither mysterious nor under my control: it popped onto my face when I saw the first snowflake of winter, and didn't go anywhere until nine months later when the sun finally came out again.

This RAWLF had graduated from college at the same time I did, but she revealed none of the discomfort of a young woman more used to hanging out at the student union than inside a boardroom. Even though she was a peer, I felt like the awkward younger sister when I was in her presence and so I kept my distance. When I walked past her desk, I would mumble and look at the floor. Perhaps she thought I watched where I walked because I was known for taking some nasty spills on the slick linoleum floors.

One day the RAWLF and I walked out of the agency for lunch at the same time. Once we were through the front doors, we immediately separated on the sidewalk. I sped up and she hung back so that there were a couple hundred yards between us. That space was filled with the sound of her high heels clicking behind me on the sidewalk and my significantly less-sexy snow boots shuffling along the cement.

Perhaps the Boston winter was tipping the scales of loneliness, or maybe each of us was simply curious to know more about the other creature. Eventually I slowed my pace and she speeded her gait until we were walking with each other.

Of course, now that I have grown into a woman with a surplus of sexiness and sophistication it seems rather silly to have been so nervous speaking to this RAWLF for the first time. I remember being quite terrified that I would let the stray cat out of the bag and reveal myself as the hick I knew myself to be. You can take the girl out of Oklahoma, but you can't completely take the Oklahoma out of the girl, and so forth, and so forth.

She asked how I liked working at the agency, and I did not venture to disclose too much.

"It's okay," I said. Then I quickly asked the same question of her.

I didn't have many friends in the office. As the youngest person in my department, most people were bosses, or people who weren't directly in charge of me but still liked to boss me around. I had assumed the RAWLF had more friends at work than she knew what to do with. Possibly because I'd never been the central point of sexual attraction in any group of people, I didn't understand that just because people wanted to sleep with a person didn't mean they wanted to spend time with that person.

"I'm not crazy about the office," she said. "When I took the job, I thought people would be friendlier."

My shuffle almost turned into a stumble; this was not the answer I had expected. The men lined up at her desk to speak to her. They spent more time brainstorming reasons to talk to her than they spent creating the campaigns they got paid for. And yet she didn't feel people were friendly; I couldn't hide my surprise.

"Really?" I asked. "I thought you were friends with everyone in the office."

She let out a very non-RAWLF-like guffaw. "Hardly," she said. "I dread coming into the office."

My morning routine consisted of waking up when my alarm went off, and staring at the ceiling for at least ten minutes while I pondered alternate options to waking up, putting on clothes, and going to an office where I would work for anywhere from eight to eighteen hours.

I dreamed of taking a taxi to Logan airport and buying a one-way ticket to, well, anywhere with a beach.

Maybe I could rewind to the days of collegiate debauchery and sit in the sorority house drinking contraband red wine in Dixie cups and smoking cigarettes on the balcony.

Wouldn't it be nice to stay in bed all day? I wondered how long it would take for someone in my office to note that I was missing—probably until that someone needed a cup of coffee.

When the RAWLF and I started to regularly go to lunch together I discovered we shared more than just our shock at the monotony of work in the real world. Lo and behold, even though at first glance she and I were as different as pecans and pumpkins, we mixed together well enough for a pretty decent piece of pie.

She was from the Northeast but still hated the winter. She wondered if everyone at work was one day away from figuring her out to be a fraud that they never should have hired in the first place. And some days her mother would call her so many times at work that she'd come over to my desk and wonder aloud if, when the time came, she'd be able to find a retirement home that didn't give the older woman phone access to the outside world.

I tried to teach her the art of self-deprecation, until I realized that a six-foot sex kitten delivering self-deprecating jokes is about as funny as a funeral.

She attempted to help my style until she realized that I was going to end up wearing whatever I found on the clearance racks at department stores no matter how many items she pointed out in the nearby boutique windows.

There was only one topic I was careful to avoid from the very beginning of our friendship: men. Since college, my dating life had been so dry I might as well have lain down on a highway in West Texas and let the sunshine pull every last drop of moisture from my body.

Even though it would have helped me sleep at night to believe this RAWLF was nothing more than a pretty face, now that she and I were friends I had to live with the knowledge that she was smart and kind, and that sometimes the universe just didn't play fair. I could imagine her tales of older men who threw their money at her in exchange for just a few moments of her afternoon, or how she used to date the best looking guy at her college but didn't really think he was that cute, or how men in a bar would line up to buy her drinks when she wasn't even thirsty.

I thought the healthiest thing for our friendship would be to avoid the topic altogether. Kind of like staying away from the donut shop when you are on a diet, it only takes one step inside to spoil everything.

And then one day, when she and I were at lunch, eating our daily serving of vegetables—mine with dressing, hers without—she brought up the topic I thought we had subliminally agreed to avoid.

"I always thought I'd be married by twenty-five," she said, as she speared a cucumber. "What happens if I don't meet someone and I have to be an old lady when I walk down the aisle? I could not live with myself if I ended up being a thirty-year-old bride."

It would be an understatement to say that I almost choked on my arugula. If I had it would have been an ironic death. Every time I say arugula it sounds like a lodged ball of phlegm is blocking all the oxygen from my throat.

"You think getting married after twenty-five is, um, old?" I asked.

"Well, of course," she said. "Doesn't everyone?"

I didn't know what to say. I mean, yes, everyone I had grown up with thought that if you were going to get married when you were older than thirty you might as well get the word "desperate" tattooed across your forehead. But that was precisely why I had marched out of my Southern sorority house and onto a plane above the Mason-Dixon line, so I could leave the marriage-is-the-only-road-to-happiness equation behind. She'd grown up in a part of the country where I thought women were expected to make their own lives. But at the end of the day, this beautiful, smart, kind woman still believed a woman had a certain age at which she became over-ripened and then spoiled, like a cantaloupe that you left sitting on your counter for too long.

"All the girls in the office who have boyfriends make me so jealous," she continued. "I'd give anything to have a good guy take me to dinner on a Saturday night."

I coiled sprouts on my fork and tried to wrap my mind around this desperation. She really did not understand that every woman in that office wished they had one-tenth of her sex appeal, or at the very least, her ability to spend eight hours in six-inch heels without going mad as a hatter. Or maybe she understood that, but felt everything positive in her life was nothing until she had a man acknowledge it.

I slowly took the white napkin from my lap, folded it into a narrow rectangle, and started to wave it above my head. It was time for me to surrender.

Geography could not protect you from the idea that you need a man to be happy.

Beauty was not a shield against loneliness.

Regular servings of arugula were doing nothing to shrink my hips.

Work wasn't cracking up to be the carnival that all the feminist magazines had promoted it to be; I enjoyed the independence of making my own living, but oftentimes the day was nothing more than stale coffee and crabby people. I could hang out all day at a DMV if I wanted that life experience.

After that day, I went back to eating pizza for lunch. The RAWLF and I still made small talk, but we never really talked again. I'd gone to all the trouble of leaving Texas, it was too heartbreaking for me to consider that I hadn't found a new state of affairs as much as I'd found all the same questions about being a woman, just wrapped in a different package.

For many years, that conversation with the RAWLF lay dormant in my brain, buried next to the names of every state capital I had memorized in high school but then decided to ignore, how to knit, and Cindy Lauper's greatest hits. But now the RAWLF's words had come back to haunt me.

My thirtieth birthday was approaching, and fast. And the back end of my twenties had brought me to a revelation. Once I'd rounded the corner of twenty-nine I'd decided that I was finally ready to go home—to Texas that is. So I packed my bags, said goodbye to Colorado, and went back in much the same way I'd left it: hopeful.

Finally I would be back in the fold of my family, and have the comforts I'd grown up around in my reach. What I'd spent so long fighting was what I found myself craving.

And the big three-oh continued to inch closer. I would wake up in the morning and feel a deep satisfaction in knowing I was home. Some things were the same as when I left, others were different. But most noticeably, everything had aged, even if just a little. I would look in the mirror and wonder the ways people could see my age on face. I wondered if they were disappointed that other parts of me hadn't changed at all. I had accepted when I moved home that my life wouldn't look like the lives of my married friends. But to know something and then to be okay with it are two separate things. For instance, I realized that I am 100 percent more likely to wear a lollipop ring than a diamond one by the time my birthday arrives. I don't feel like an old maid, but occasionally, quietly, I do wonder if I am passing my prime.

Now I loudly wonder if I've momentarily gone crazy—should I define my prime years as the ones when a hypothetical man would hypothetically be most attracted to me?

Do I listen to the feminists?

Do I listen to the Betty Crockers?

Do I step out on a limb from the conversations happening with working women at happy hours, stay-at-home moms around playgrounds, and the warriors who fight to keep one foot in both sandboxes and stop categorizing people based on how closely their lives mirror a traditional female existence?

Does the fact that I'm ready to admit that I don't have anything figured out mean that I am finally growing up?

Doesn't it make sense to just stop with the have-nots and simply be happy?

I have friends with successful careers and no significant relationship, as well as friends who have successful relationships but never developed careers. There are people more like me, who at different times in their twenties have either had successful relationships or successful careers. These women live in all the cities I've adopted for either short or long periods of time in the last decade. Big cities, small cities, red states, blue states.

State lines don't seem to change the struggle.

Party lines don't make a dent in the debates.

No panty lines will paint a prettier picture but does not have a direct effect on what is true.

You must accept my sincerest apology if you are a woman who falls outside this sweeping stereotype and have found a way to juggle all eight million things that matter to you without alienating friends, family, lovers, and bosses at one point or another. But as a woman who was raised with the idea that the world was at my fingertips, that anything I wanted could be mine for the taking, on the eve of my thirtieth birthday I am ready to stand up and say that trying to have it all is not all it's cracked up to be.

Unfortunately, that announcement is not going to make turning thirty any easier to handle. If it took me all of my twenties to make a realization that should have been intuitive, it might take me to the end of my thirties to learn how to apply that lesson to my life. What will rise to the top of my priorities? Which things will matter the most?

Some days I wonder if turning thirty would feel less shaky if I had a better indication about how it would feel to actually wake up, look at the calendar, and know that from that day forward a two would never be the first number in my age. I tried asking friends who had already turned thirty how it felt and the answers I got were vague at best, condescending at worst.

"It doesn't feel very different," one friend said. Which would be an acceptable answer if the word "very" was something quantifiable. Are we using "very" as in "I love you very much, so much I would walk on coals for you," or are we talking more of a "I enjoy very spicy foods" from a Midwesterner who thinks ketchup's got a lot of kick.

Other friends have opined that my birthday would be here soon enough and then I'd know how thirty feels. Perhaps I wouldn't have minded this brush-off if I didn't know for a fact these same people were the ones nervously knocking their knee-high boots together when they were approaching thirty. They had to remember the fear, yet they weren't willing to help appease mine.

It's like I'm starting my period for the first time all over again: the onset of menstruation was the only other time in my life I recall feeling so alone while waiting for such a universal change to occur.

Unfortunately for my innately adolescent need to know that I was just as normal as everyone else, I was the late bloomer in my group of friends. If you believe doctors, this delay was due to genetics. If you prefer to listen to the hippies, it was because I didn't live in a house positioned directly under a power line or eat lots of hormone-injected cows for dinner.

All around me, my friends were getting their periods. And predictably, each one joined this biological club in the same way: one day she was happy to cluster at the lunch table with all of us non-menstruators and hypothesize on how it would feel when it happened and the next day she would show up at school with an air of mystery and maturity that none of us could duplicate.

The numbers at my lunch table dwindled, and eventually became a noon-time party for me, myself, and I. Everyone else knew what it felt like to step to the other side, but I was left wondering whether the leap would make me feel sick, or elated, or if it would be an odd combination of both—like when my neighbor and I had stolen one of her dad's beers and shared it behind the garage so we could see what all the fuss was about.

Weeks went by and I waited, and waited, and waited some more. I wondered if every twinge in my belly was the wheel of my reproductive organs finally starting to turn. Every hunger pain, every nervous sensation was a reason for me to speed to the nearest bathroom and check my underwear for any evidence of womanhood.

I'd ask my girlfriends how it felt to be one step closer to grown-up and they couldn't articulate whether they liked it or hated it.

I'd ask my mom what to expect and she would sketch a picture of a woman's uterus.

Finally, I realized that I could ask all kinds of questions but the answers wouldn't matter. Even if I hated having my period, once it arrived I was going to be stuck with monthly menstruation (as far as I knew) forever. (My mother had neglected to draw me a picture of menopause.)

So I sat and I waited and eventually it arrived. By my second cycle I was sick of it and wished it away. Then in my twenties I had a couple months where I made bargains with the good Lord above if it would Just Show Up Already. Now I have dear friends who pay thousands of dollars in an effort to make a baby and miss a period. Isn't that so true of life. We want it, want it, want it—and then we want the opposite.

CALL ME THE BIRTHDAY GIRL

You just can't do much to force nature, it's going to take due course in its own due time.

The opposite of learning that I couldn't speed up nature taught me that I couldn't do anything to reverse it either.

Which is exactly what it was like to face my thirtieth birthday. I'd wanted to get older until I hit my late twenties, and then I started wishing for the whole damn process to just slow down.

When the birthday chatter in my brain reached a fever pitch, I called my mother to talk about turning thirty. Well, in all honesty, part of me wanted counsel and comfort, another part of me wanted to make sure she knew how to access my wish list on amazon.com. Drawing me a picture of a birthday cake wasn't going to cut it.

After I explained that my upcoming birthday was causing me great stress, she very calmly asked me what had me so out of whack.

"Because thirty is old," I said.

"Older than fifty-four?" she asked, with all fifty-four years of her wisdom intact.

She asked if I remembered the day after my graduation from college. Of course I didn't. I barely even remembered my graduation ceremony on account of the Bloody Marys I'd drank with friends before we even stepped into our gowns.

She wanted to know if I could recall the day after my high school prom. I couldn't.

The day after I started my first job? No.

The day after I moved into my first apartment on my own? Not really. Okay, not at all.

My mother was talking about me growing up. And unlike many of the conversations we'd had on the subject, this one did not provoke any profound embarrassment on my part. No nude baby pictures had to be shown to strangers for her to explain that the days we grow up are rarely the days that are designated for growing up.

She explained that a monumental day didn't make the day that comes after it feel a whole lot different from the one that had come before. The real changes happen on the anonymous days wedged between the monumental ones that are recorded on video cameras and preserved in photo albums.

I understood what she was saying. For example, there were no pictures of the very first day I had to haul myself out of bed with a massive hangover and go to a lecture class even though I thought it might kill me. But that day was more defining than the one when I walked across the stage for my diploma, because the day I dragged myself out of bed was the day I decided the college party scene was not going to keep me from a career. On that day I did a lot of growing up.

I was in my mid-twenties when my parents moved to Malaysia for a few years. It was a good move for my father's career, and also a good move for their marriage. They found a quick fix for empty-nest syndrome: Simply build a new nest on the opposite side of the world.

When my mom and I were on the phone that day she told me a story I'd never heard before. My parents lived in a small town, in a rented condominium on the top floor of a high-rise. They didn't choose the top floor because they wanted to act like high rollers or because they had always dreamed of living in a penthouse. On the contrary, the sole reason they wanted that unit was because it came with a rooftop garden where you could sit out at night and watch the sun sink into the sea.

Even though everyone said it was a futile effort in the Malaysian climate, my mother insisted on potted plants for the patio. Every day she would go into the heat and water those plants. The routine was the same. She'd load up two pails of water and carry them outside with her, carefully placing a wedge in the door that led to the roof so it wouldn't close. Time and again she reminded herself that if the door shut it would automatically lock. Because the door was the only way off the roof, if it ever locked behind her she would be trapped.

After my parents had been living in the building for a few months—which is just long enough for a false sense of familiarity to settle into your daily routine—my mother went out one morning around ten to water her plants. My father was at work and she said she was enjoying a quiet morning, letting her brain work through some day-to-day problems she had been dwelling on.

As the human mind so often likes to do, her mind was working so hard on the big things, it skipped over the one small detail of wedging the door open. Her flip-flops were clapping against the cement and she was lugging the heavy pails to the far side of the patio when she heard the click of the door. She didn't even have to turn around to know what had happened—she was stuck on top of the roof.

My mother didn't panic. In fact, for the first twenty minutes, she acted as though it were any other morning on the patio. She watered the plants, and pulled a few errant weeds from the pots.

Once the plants were watered, she began to think through her options. Of course, that was when it occurred to her that she probably shouldn't have used all the water on the plants—in the seven hours before my father arrived home from work and presumably found her on the roof there was a very good chance she would need that hydration.

The days in Malaysia were even warmer than what they had known in Texas. She often used the word "relentless" to describe the heat they woke to on the other side of the world.

As the sun rose toward noon, the shade on the roof quickly started to disappear. She was wearing a sleeveless camisole and a pair of walking shorts; it wasn't long before she could feel her skin burning. The sliver of shade she had been sitting in completely went away and she began to wonder if she was sitting in the middle of a much larger crisis than she had first realized.

My parents' little town was safe, so there was no need for the physical force of a guard, but the building hired one anyway. His name was Sonny. The main point of his presence was to remind stray dogs and the occasional stray person that they should wander elsewhere.

During his shifts, Sonny prayed with a long strand of beads. When I visited my parents, every time I looked into the office where Sonny sat, I'd see him praying with those beads. There are days when I have trouble concentrating long enough to send a text message, and this man spends ten hours a day on the same length of beads.

When my mom really started to worry about the heat, she walked to the edge of the balcony and leaned over, yelling Sonny's name. But she was so far up that the wind took her voice away. She was sure no one on the ground could hear her. And so she returned to the place where she had been resting and lay down on the cement.

Without anything to do but worry, she decided that instead she would pray, like Sonny did. Slowly, she started to click through every worry on her mind, constantly having to pull herself away from the most immediate worry of the heat, the suffocating heat, and when she would have relief. She prayed until she started to feel drowsy. The heat was closing in on her chest and in her brain. But she clicked through item after item, attaching prayer after prayer to different people, different thoughts.

Eventually my mother passed out.

She woke up to two hands lifting her off the ground by her shoulders. The hands were large and strong, and when she looked to the right she saw the string of prayer beads that belonged to Sonny wrapped around his wrist and the set of master keys to the building in his palm. When she turned her head she saw the profile of Sonny's face.

CALL ME THE BIRTHDAY GIRL

"I am so hot," she said to Sonny. And he said that she kept saying that over and over and over again. "I am so hot. I am so hot. I am so hot."

Later he explained to my father that all during his morning prayers, every bead he clicked off had made him look up. He kept looking up, looking up, and then he realized that every time he was looking up he was actually looking to my mother and father's apartment. He hadn't seen my mother all day, he realized. And usually she left for errands in the morning. He did not want to bother her, but the need to make sure she was okay weighed heavy on his heart.

He knocked on the door and she did not answer, so he and the superintendent decided that someone should check on that strange creature who thought the heat of Malaysia could be tamed enough for plants to turn into flowers.

My mother does not remember the day she moved into her apartment, or when she hit the one- or two-year anniversary of living there. But she told me that the first day she felt she was at home in Malaysia was that day when Sonny missed seeing her around, went to investigate, and saved my mother from heatstroke, or worse, on that roof. It was the day she finally started to see how Asia would change her, that all these people had something to teach her.

My mother said I should stop looking at one particular day as a starting point for being older.

"The crow's feet don't know which day you actually turn a year older," she pointed out, "they show up on the days when you start to worry like an old woman."

"Okay," I said, "I'll remember that."

Then we said our goodbyes, hung up the phone, and I ran to my bathroom mirror to do a close-up inspection to make sure that my worries over this birthday hadn't already done irreparable damage.

With ten days until my birthday and strict marching orders from my mother not to spend those ten days worrying about turning thirty, I found myself wondering what the most appropriate way to say goodbye to my twenties would be.

I could open up a bottle of wine and start to go through the archives of digital photos on my computer.

I could take up a hobby that is a manifestation of maturity, like golf.

I could scroll through the contacts on my phone and start calling everyone I know, telling them one reason I appreciated their presence in my life over the last decade.

Or I could do something that would not give me a physical and mental hangover, involve the use of heavy, iron clubs in an emotionally charged time of my life, or cause the people in my phone book to wonder if I was having trouble managing medications: I could go and visit my grandmother. Now that it finally didn't involve flying, it was as simple as saying that: I could go and visit my grandmother. No airplanes or reservations or rental cars needed.

Whenever I meet new people one of the first things I try to figure out is if they are the kind of people who move around a lot, or the sort of people who stay one place for long periods of time. I was raised in a sampling of cities in the South, and since college have lived in seven other cities. My grandma often says that she writes down my addresses in pencil, on account of me changing them again before the ink would even have time to dry. On the other hand, if I could write in blood without fainting from seeing a prick in my finger, that's what I would have used to write my grandma's address.

I was nothin' more than a tadpole on a monitor when my grandma bought her house in East Texas, moved in all her antique furniture, and announced to anyone who'd listen—the hummingbirds, some armadillos, and my grandpa, assuming he hadn't turned his hearing aid off to avoid hearing any more instructions

CALL ME THE BIRTHDAY GIRL

on how to carry my grandma's antique furniture—that she wasn't leaving that house until they carried her out in a casket.

I have suspicions that none of the furniture in her house has been rearranged since her first day there. I imagine that my grandmother works the vacuum into most of those hard-to-reach places, but I reckon that under some of the heavier pieces there are enough allergens to induce a countywide epidemic of hay fever.

In this way, driving to my grandmother's house is like driving to the one location that has been consistent throughout my entire life. It's as emotionally predictable as getting on the phone with an old boyfriend, where you know that you are going to start off excited, then get nostalgic, but then get really annoyed and uber-pissed off when he makes a comment that reminds you of every reason you broke up with him the first time around.

Except my grandma doesn't make me really annoyed or uber-pissed off. With her I go straight from nostalgia to the deep satisfaction that comes with your stomach being so full you wish for elastic waistbands to come back in style—so your pants could simply grow outward in proportion with your happiness—the instant I walk through her door all of my favorite foods magically materialize.

Of course, there are parts of visiting my grandma's house that have changed through the years. As she and my grandpa have gotten older, instead of bringing glasses of iced tea to the driveway as soon as one of our cars pulled in front of the house, she waits with a tray in the kitchen. She also got a dog about seven years ago—once she realized that getting older wasn't inspiring her to feel more affinity for the human race.

And the most recent change that will forever alter my arrival at Grandma's house—the diagnosis of my grandfather as a sufferer of Alzheimer's. When my grandmother lost her breasts to cancer, I think she believed that disease had taken all it could from the family. Unfortunately, that was not the case.

But on the day that I visit my grandparents to say hello, the air is not full of fading memories. The blessing of living in East Texas is that once July rolls around it's too hot to think about much except what time the sun's going down and how the hell you are going to get your armpits to stop sweating.

"I imagine," my grandmother says as soon as I see her face at the top of her staircase, "that I'll be able to adjust to hell in five minutes after spending my life sweating in Texas."

My grandfather is sleeping in his favorite recliner, the one I used to hang from while he leaned it back and then popped it forward so that I could play like I was a monkey in the Amazon. (Tough to make an argument against me being a genius in the making when you hear about the ole' monkey in the Amazon game, isn't it?)

My grandma and I tiptoe past him on our way to the kitchen where I take a seat next to the iced tea and pecan praline treats she has set out for me. She immediately gets back to cooking more of the food that will likely cause a nervous breakdown the next time I put on a bikini.

"Your mother says you think you're old because you're turning thirty," she starts off.

Silly me, I was thinking we could start off with a subject that didn't make me feel quite as sensitive, like, say, the fact that in the last three years I hadn't met a man I wanted to go on more than three dates with.

"I'm glad that she called to roll out the red carpet for my arrival," I said.

"No, no, no," Grandma corrected me, "I called her because I knew I didn't have enough bourbon balls to get you tipsy enough to talk," she said.

I looked at the counter, then at the floor.

"I'm actually trying not to think about the birthday anymore. Mom told me to stop focusing on the big days, and just live the ones in between."

My grandma had been facing the counter as she sliced fruit for an ambrosia, but she turned to face me, knife pointing outward.

"Did she tell you the story about being trapped on the roof in Malaysia?"

"You know," I said. "I had never heard that one. I was surprised because I was expecting the one about Dad getting punched in the face on the night of his bachelor party, and then showing up at their wedding with a black eye."

My grandma cocked her head to one side, "That makes sense," she said. "The bachelor party story is more for patience-in-the-face-of-the-unexpected. The Malaysia roof story is an enjoy-every-minute-because-you-don't-know-when-it-will-be-your-last."

My grandma does not talk to me about my grandpa's condition. As far as I know, she does not talk about it to anyone except the doctors. But there are times in conversation when what's unspoken is the most palpable presence in the room, like the worst kind of humidity you could ever imagine, pushing you down to the ground in a search for cooler air—just one second when you can breathe without painful awareness of the struggle.

I lean back in my chair and think about what to say next.

"Did I tell you about when I saw David?" I ask.

Most of my stories of my brother are from when we are young and I did things like make him eat mud and play house with me, and, well, is it really a surprise that once he got old enough to be able to avoid hanging out with me, he did?

David was still exploring his twenties, and had recently moved to Brooklyn so he could live in a loft with other skateboarders. As any overbearing sister who pays due respect to her maternal urges would do, I'd ventured to New York City to make sure "loft" was not code for "hole in the wall where I sleep and also grow marijuana plants."

I had found that his bedroom was, quite literally, a hole cut into the wall of a larger apartment. But since there were no marijuana plants in sight, I decided against stuffing him in my suitcase and taking him home with me. And instead I bought him meals that did not originate in a taqueria.

My brother insists that he can subsist wholly on a diet of burritos. It is my grandma's largest grievance with his lifestyle. My brother argues that a burrito offers a food from each of the four food groups. My grandma believes that a meal should be composed of distinct and independent parts, a little like the United States government.

I told her that I saw—with my own two eyes—David eat a meal that had an appetizer and a side order of vegetables in addition to the entrée. And that none of these disparate parts had been scooped together into a tortilla.

After our meal, my brother and I had gone for a walk in the streets of New York City, which was more than a little strange for me. The walk had given me the distinct feeling that Manhattan had become the blue Schwinn bicycle that I learned to ride first and then passed down to him, except he had taken the two wheels that had terrified me for so long and immediately learned how to jump them over curbs and speed down the road.

As I was contemplating this big thought about how our lives were intersecting as we aged, suddenly my brother had said, "You know what I love about New York City?"

I explained to my grandma that I thought David and I were about to have a significant moment, the kind of moment that would prove our deep bond as sister and brother.

But he had looked at me and raised his eyebrows and said, "Puer-to Ri-can women." Then he stopped walking and turned

CALL ME THE BIRTHDAY GIRL

around to look at the Puerto Rican woman who had just passed. "I'd never seen women so beautiful until I moved to this city."

My grandma laughed for a second, but then asked why in heaven's name I'd thought to tell that story.

"I thought it would be nice for you to know that at least one person in the family is having a good time right now."

"What makes you think I'm not having a good time?" she asked.

I'd thought the answer to that question was obvious.

"I just thought, with Grandpa being sick and all . . . " I trailed off.

"Considering you think a thirtieth birthdays is something to be sad about," she said, but then she apologized if that sounded harsh. "How do I explain to you," she wondered, "that there is something good in every day? You are here with us today, and that is good."

Until that moment I had always imagined that to bear witness to someone's life was something that entailed a commitment between a man and a woman. I imagined that my grandma would become my grandpa's memory when he lost his because she had stood with him in a church and committed to be by his side for all of their time.

And I'd been worried that the older I got without meeting someone special to spend my life with, that my life would go without witness, which was essentially like it wasn't happening at all.

But people were bearing witness to my life. My brother. My mother. My father. My grandmother. And in exchange, I was bearing witness for them.

When I finally stepped across the finish line of my second decade I would do it with a pocket mirror in my purse. So that when it was all said and done I could take it out and see my reflection. So I could continue to bear witness to my own progression.

Maybe with crow's feet, maybe without.

Maybe with wrinkles that would embarrass any self-respecting RAWLF, maybe without.

But definitely with the shadows of people I care for standing behind me, reminding me to be thankful of another day, in whatever package it arrives in.

My grandma put down her knife. "I don't feel like cooking anymore right now," she said.

The praline I had been chewing got lodged for a second in my throat, its path stunted by surprise.

"What do you want to do?" I asked.

"I'd like for you to take three glasses of iced tea onto the porch, and I'm going to wake your grandpa up and bring him outside with us," she said.

And just like that, the three of us ended up on the patio, watching a sunset on an anonymous day that I'll most likely remember until the end of my life.

Acknowledgments

I would never dream of answering to "ma'am," but I am old enough to be one and so there are many people to thank.

Thank you, thank you, thank you to Lauren Shults, my agent, and Brooke Warner, my editor. These two amazing women made this book happen.

My friendship with Karen Pfaff was the best thing that came out of my advertising years, and even though it was a tumultuous decade, I still think it was worth the trade. Anne Ferraro, Jen Weinberg, Cat McCadden, and Caleb Wills were all blessings brought to me from wildly different zip codes.

Will Clarke, Anna Gregory, Jane Brody Koenke, and David Register were creative directors in advertising who gave me direction worth following in life. Andrew Snyder was not around for the making of this book, but I give thanks that he finally showed up on the scene—I'd go another thirty years if he'd be waiting at the finish.

There's little chance my dad or brother made it through all the bikini wax stories to get this far in the book, but in case you flip back here, I am blessed to count you both as friends.

And to the woman who taught me the beauty of being yourself. Grandma, I love you big like Alaska.

About the Author

©JAKE DEAN

Anna Mitchael began her writing career by instructing patrons of her lemonade stand to buy some "or else." She continued to threaten people for nearly a decade as an advertising copywriter, making the publication of her first book the only time she's ever told the truth in print. She is a reformed nomad who recently returned home to Texas. She will tolerate "y'all" but reserves the right to raise hell when anyone calls her "ma'am."

Read more of her writing at www.annamitchael.com.

Selected Titles from Seal Press

For more than thirty years, Seal Press has published groundbreaking books. By women. For women. Visit our website at www.sealpress.com. Check out the Seal Press blog at www.sealpress.com/blog.

The Choice Effect: Love and Commitment in an Age of Too Many Options, by Amalia McGibbon, Lara Vogel, and Claire A. Williams. $16.95, 978-1-58005-293-1. Three young, successful, and ambitious women provide insight into the quarterlife angst that surrounds dating and relationships and examine why more options equals less commitment for today's twentysomethings.

Click: Young Women on the Moments That Made Them Feminists, edited by Courtney E. Martin and J. Courtney Sullivan. $16.95, 978-1-58005-285-6. Notable writers and celebrities entertain and illuminate with true stories recalling the distinct moments when they knew they were feminists.

Gringa: A Contradictory Girlhood, by Melissa Hart. $16.95, 978-1-58005-294-8. This coming-of-age memoir offers a touching, reflective look at one girl's struggle with the dichotomies of class, culture, and sexuality.

Rockabye: From Wild to Child, by Rebecca Woolf. $15.95, 978-1-58005-232-0. The coming-of-age story of a rock n' roll party girl who becomes unexpectedly pregnant, decides to keep the baby, and discovers motherhood on her own terms.

Valencia, by Michelle Tea. $14.95, 978-1-58005-238-2. A fast-paced account of one girl's search for love and high times in the dyke world of San Francisco. By turns poetic and frantic, Valencia is a visceral ride through the queer girl underground of the Mission.

Chick Flick Road Kill: A Behind the Scenes Odyssey into Movie-Made America, by Alicia Rebensdorf. $15.95, 978-1-58005-194-1. A twentysomething's love-hate relationship with picture-perfect Hollywood sends her on a road trip in search of a more real America.